DEPARTMENT OF THE NAVY
HEADQUARTERS UNITED STATES MARINE CORPS
3000 MARINE CORPS PENTAGON
WASHINGTON, DC 20350-3000

MARINE CORPS SUBSTANCE ABUSE PROGRAM

DEPARTMENT OF THE NAVY
HEADQUARTERS UNITED STATES MARINE CORPS
3000 MARINE CORPS PENTAGON
WASHINGTON, DC 20350-3000

MCO 5300.17
MRC-4
11 Apr 2011

MARINE CORPS ORDER 5300.17

From: Commandant of the Marine Corps
To: Distribution List

Subj: MARINE CORPS SUBSTANCE ABUSE PROGRAM

Ref: (a) MCO 1200.17B
(b) 10 U.S.C. Ch. 41 (UCMJ)
(c) Manual for Courts-Martial 2008
(d) MCO P1900.16F
(e) SECNAVINST 5300.28D
(f) MCO 1070.12K
(g) MCO 1610.7F
(h) BUMEDINST 5300.8
(i) SECNAV M-5210.1
(j) MCO 6320.2E
(k) 42 U.S.C. Sec 290dd-2
(l) 42 C.F.R. Sec 2.1
(m) 21 U.S.C. Sec 801, et. seq., (Controlled Substances Act)

Encl: (1) Marine Corps Substance Abuse Program Policy

1. Situation. To provide policy and procedural guidance to commanders, substance abuse personnel, and Marines in order to effectively utilize and execute the Marine Corps Substance Abuse Program, per references (a) through (m). This Order provides both policy and guidance to commanders so that they may improve their capability to treat and prevent alcohol and drug abuse problems that detract from unit performance and mission readiness.

2. Cancellation. MCO P1700.24B and MCO 5355.4.

3. Mission. Commanders are tasked with the implementation of the program established in this Order. All installation Substance Abuse Programs shall be in compliance with the policies and procedures contained in enclosure (1). Key program elements are prevention, timely identification, education and/or treatment, appropriate discipline, or other administrative

DISTRIBUTION STATEMENT A: Approved for public release; distribution is unlimited.

actions followed by either restoration to full duty or separation, as appropriate.

4. Execution

a. Commander's Intent and Concept of Operations

(1) Commander's Intent. To ensure all individuals who are tasked with assisting Marines and their families with substance abuse issues are provided adequate information pertaining to all policies, procedures, responsibilities, and technical instructions.

(2) Concept of Operations. This Order should be used in conjunction with references (a) through (m) to ensure compliance with policies and procedures established by the Commandant of the Marine Corps (CMC) and higher headquarters.

b. Coordinating Instructions. This Order was extracted and completely reorganized from a previous Personal Services Order, and contains substantial changes.

5. Administration and Logistics

a. The currency, accuracy, and completeness of publication and distribution of this Order, and changes thereto, are the responsibility of the Deputy Commandant, Manpower and Reserve Affairs, Behavioral Health Branch (HQMC) (MRC-4).

b. Maintenance of this Order is the command's responsibility.

c. Recommendations for changes to this Order should be submitted to (HQMC) (MRC-4) via the appropriate chain of command.

d. Records created as a result of this directive shall include records management requirements to ensure the proper maintenance and use of records, regardless of format or medium, to promote accessibility and authorized retention per the approved records schedule and reference (i).

6. Command and Signal

a. Command. This Order is applicable to the Marine Corps Active duty and Reserve component.

b. <u>Signal</u>. This Order is effective on the date signed.

R. E. MILSTEAD JR
Deputy Commandant for
Manpower and Reserve Affairs

DISTRIBUTION: 10207760800

LOCATOR SHEET

Subj: MARINE CORPS SUBSTANCE ABUSE PROGRAM

Location: ____
(Indicate location(s) of copy(ies) of this Order.)

RECORD OF CHANGES

Log completed change action as indicated.

Change Number	Date of Change	Date Entered	Signature of Person Incorporating Change

TABLE OF CONTENTS

Chapter 1

Substance Abuse Roles and Responsibilities

1. General

a. Alcohol abuse and the distribution, possession, use, trafficking or distribution of illegal drugs or drug paraphernalia is contrary to the effective performance of Marines and to the Marine Corps mission, and will not be tolerated. Alcohol and drug offenses must and will be dealt with swiftly and effectively.

b. The wrongful use, possession, manufacture, distribution, or introduction onto a military installation, vessel, vehicle, or aircraft used by or under the control of the armed forces by any person subject to this Order, of a controlled substance analogue or a designer drug is prohibited.

c. The wrongful use, possession, manufacture, distribution, or introduction onto a military installation, vessel, vehicle, or aircraft used by or under the control of the armed forces by any person subject to this Order, of natural substances (e.g. fungi), chemicals (e.g. chemicals wrongfully used as inhalants), propellants, or prescribed or over-the-counter drugs or pharmaceutical compounds with the intent to induce intoxication, excitement, or stupefaction of their own central nervous system, or that of another, is prohibited.

d. Paragraphs 1b. and 1c. above are punitive and any violations may result in prosecution under reference (b) and/or adverse administrative action.

e. The Marine Corps Substance Abuse Program shall be administered in accordance with this Order. The objective of this Order is to improve the capability of Commanders, substance abuse personnel, and Marines in preventing and treating alcohol and drug abuse problems that detract from unit performance and mission readiness.

2. Roles and Responsibilities

a. The CMC, Personal and Family Readiness Division (MR) shall:

(1) Develop and recommend Service plans and policy for substance abuse prevention and treatment.

(2) Coordinate the Substance Abuse Program with CMC (ARDB) Records Management, Major Commands, other Headquarters, HQMC staff agencies, and higher headquarters.

(3) Develop a budget through the Program Objective Memorandum (POM) to support installation prevention plans.

(4) Publish a long-range, integrated plan for Substance Abuse Prevention, including training for prevention staff, Substance Abuse Counselors and unit Substance Abuse personnel. The "integrated plan" will target negative behaviors exacerbated by alcohol misuse and drug abuse. The plan will include an integrated delivery system supported by funding, training curricula and materials, measures of effectiveness and evaluation, and support staff.

(5) Sponsor Military Occupational Specialty (MOS) 0149, Substance Abuse Control Officer/Specialist (SACO/S).

(6) Participate as an augmentee on the Inspector General's Inspection Program, to ensure compliance with service standards for the substance abuse functional area (FA 200).

(7) Attend, and as appropriate, host organizational conferences and working groups pertaining to the Substance Abuse Program, and provide information to command activities.

(8) Ensure substance abuse programs are included in the Headquarters Marine Corps (HQMC) Mobilization and Contingency Plan.

(9) Conduct research and provide evidence-based models to support identified needs within unit prevention programs and installation treatment services. Evaluate programs and services with both quantitative and qualitative data.

(10) Provide guidelines to be used as Performance Outcome Measures for evaluation purposes.

(11) Administer central programs and training when in the best interest of the Marine Corps.

(12) Track alcohol abuse and drug abuse trends in the Marine Corps and periodically publish "lessons learned" and other resources to assist commanders in risk management.

b. <u>The CMC, Public Affairs (PA) shall</u>:

(1) Coordinate with CMC (MR) to ensure key themes, events, and updates regarding the Marine Corps Substance Abuse Program are incorporated into the Annual PA Plan.

(2) Disseminate information on key Marine Corps Substance Abuse themes, events and updates through MCNEWS, Marines Magazine, and civilian media outlets, as appropriate and consistent with the Privacy Act.

(3) Coordinate with CMC (MR) to obtain information and/or provide a subject matter expert as spokesperson when responding to civilian media inquiries pertaining to the Marine Corps Substance Abuse Program, consistent with the Privacy Act.

(4) Coordinate with command Public Affairs Officers (PAOs) to ensure information on Corps-wide Substance Abuse Program themes, events, and updates are provided for incorporation into the local command information effort.

c. The CG, Marine Forces Command, Marine Forces Pacific, Marine Forces Reserve and Logistics Command shall:

(1) Designate and maintain staff cognizance on all matters pertaining to the Substance Abuse Program, policies, and associated resources for subordinate commands.

(2) Conduct inspections of Substance Abuse Programs to ensure compliance with this Order.

(3) Review, prioritize and consolidate POM requirements concerning personnel, budget and training initiatives for Substance Abuse Programs.

(4) Ensure Substance Abuse Programs are included in the appropriate Mobilization and Contingency Plans.

d. The installation commander shall implement and maintain Substance Abuse Programs to meet the needs of the tenant commands.

e. The MCCS Director shall:

(1) Establish a Substance Abuse Counseling Center (SACC) under the direct supervision of the Behavioral Health Programs Director.

(2) Ensure all Commanders and Sergeants Major down to battalion/squadron levels or recruiting district/station levels,

as appropriate, receive a brief on the Substance Abuse Program within 45 days of assuming command or position.

(3) Validate data through quarterly audits to ensure accuracy of reports submitted to higher headquarters.

(4) Ensure a Quality Assurance (QA) Program is implemented in accordance with chapter 5 of this Order, which, at a minimum, includes a needs assessment, client care evaluations, credentials review and privileging, resource management, and follow-up.

(5) Develop personnel, training, logistics, facilities, and budget requirements relative to the POM for all Substance Abuse Programs.

(6) Conduct inspections of Substance Abuse Programs to ensure compliance with the program standards and policies established in this Order.

(7) Ensure the Substance Abuse Program is included in the Installation Contingency and Mobilization Plan to support rapid development of additional fiscal, logistical, and human resource requirements in times of emergency, mobilization, large-scale deployment, repatriation, or evacuation.

(8) Ensure Substance Abuse Program themes, events, and updates are incorporated into public affairs planning and products, consistent with the Privacy Act.

f. Commanders shall:

(1) Be fully involved in the Substance Abuse Program, in order to enhance personal and family readiness.

(2) Ensure the prevention and intervention requirements in this Order are met.

(3) Refer service members within their command to prevention and intervention services, referring all service members involved in an alcohol related incident, positive drug urinalysis, or admission of illegal drug use for screening.

(4) Designate a SACO/S to perform the functions identified by this Order and any additional relevant local installation Order(s).

g. SACO/S. Commanders will appoint in writing a SACO/S, MOS 0149, for a minimum of one year. Training for this MOS is through a HQMC (MRC-4)-approved course and shall be completed within 90 days of appointment. Commanders must ensure candidates for this billet meet the requirements of reference (a). Consideration is given to maturity, grade, and prior experience. It is inappropriate to appoint a Marine whose beliefs are inconsistent with the goals of the Substance Abuse Program or who experienced alcohol or domestic problems within two years of assignment. A Marine assigned as a SACO/S, who is recovering from alcohol or drug dependence, will have a minimum of two years sobriety or abstinence, and a strong personal recovery program. Unit SACO duties include:

(1) Advising the commander on all substance abuse matters.

(2) Identifying and conducting administrative reviews of available records and documents, and referring alcohol or drug abusers to the SACC via the commander for screening.

(3) Maintaining accurate records on Marines with alcohol or drug problems. For information on SACO records, see chapter 3, page 3-14, paragraph 13.a. of this Order.

(4) Regarding drug testing, it is essential that the SACO accomplishes the following:

(a) Ensures screening of all Marines annually, regardless of rank, for the presence of drugs. Additionally, unit commanders will direct the SACO to test at least ten percent of their population monthly. Ensures urinalysis samples are properly prepared and shipped for testing. Most common discrepancies include missing chain-of-custody documents and incorrect test premise codes.

(b) Views drug testing results in the Internet Forensic Toxicology Drug Testing Laboratory (IFTDTL) portal after every test;

(c) Prints testing outcome and notifies the commander of the results;

(d) Prepares the drug testing determination memo for the commander; and

(e) Coordinates with medical to accomplish the Medical Officer's (MO) review of all drug positives, and coordinates and provides all pertinent drug use information to the commander for further submission to the Drug Demand Reduction Coordinator (DDRC) or SACC.

(5) Conducts annual unit substance abuse prevention education.

(6) Displays substance abuse prevention materials from the SACC in common areas.

(7) Monitors Marines in the command aftercare program, and provides the commander with bi-weekly progress updates on adherence to the aftercare plan provided by the local SACC.

h. SACC Director. The SACC Director reports directly to the Behavioral Health Programs Director and is responsible for the day-to-day operation of the SACC and its staff. The SACC Director will:

(1) Establish and maintain a detailed Standard Operating Procedure documenting the SACC operation.

(2) Ensure installation SACCs obtain and maintain accreditation through the Commission on Accreditation of Rehabilitation Facilities or the Joint Commission, formerly the Joint Commission on the Accreditation of Healthcare Organizations (for installations co-joined with hospital treatment programs). Copies of accreditation certificates shall be forwarded to HQMC (MRC-4).

(3) Provide correspondence between the SACC and the command regarding a Marine's screening, treatment and aftercare status.

(4) Submit all substance abuse information when requested, (e.g., from the Alcohol and Drug Management Information Tracking System (ADMITS). Together with the Behavioral Health Programs Director, the SACC Director is responsible for data accuracy.

(5) Ensure referred Marines receive services to address individualized needs identified in the treatment plan using a continuum of care and a case management system.

(6) Ensure monthly training is provided to the SACO/S on referral and treatment issues, and upon request assist SACOs with providing substance abuse education to Marines in their command, to include assistance with lesson plan development.

(7) Provide substance abuse prevention and treatment information and awareness training to all Marines aboard their installation.

(8) Ensure Marines are informed there is no strict confidentiality of communication between the counselor and Marine since the counselor must disclose criminal activity, threats to harm self or others, child abuse and neglect, and other significant matters to the unit commander. Ensure Marines sign and are provided a copy of the "Confidentiality of Client Records," NAVMC 11689. All forms referred to in this Order can be found at the following website: https://navalforms.daps.dla.mil

(9) Ensure treatment is conducted by qualified personnel (e.g., Alcohol and Drug Counselor (ADC)-II certified Substance Abuse Counselors, physicians, and psychologists credentialed and privileged through the Naval Hospital), meeting specific treatment requirements. Ensure Navy ADC-II counselor certification is obtained within 90 days of hire and a copy of this certification is submitted to HQMC (MRC-4).

(10) Provide administrative and clinical supervision and ongoing training to counselors to ensure quality services are provided in accordance with current policy.

(11) Assemble an Interdisciplinary Team (IDT) at least weekly to determine treatment admission and/or discharge, and to review the Marine's progress. See chapter 3, paragraph 2.f. of this Order.

(12) Establish a tobacco-free workplace, congruent with SECNAVINST 5100.13E, "Navy and Marine Corps Tobacco Policy."

i. Medical Officer (MO). Treatment will be provided under the supervision of the MO (physician or clinical psychologist credentialed and privileged through the Naval Hospital) assigned by the local Medical Treatment Facility (MTF). The MO is appointed to support the continuum of care. The MO will be responsible for authorizing any treatment changes, to include: discharge, making diagnosis, determining portal of entry for Marines entering the continuum of care, and approving Individual Treatment Plans (ITP).

j. Alcohol Abuse Prevention Specialist (AAPS). The Installation/Depot Commander will assign an AAPS, which may be an additional duty assigned to an installation SACC Substance

Abuse Counselor. All AAPSs will complete the Certified Prevention Specialist course at the Naval School of Health Sciences, within 180 days of assignment. The AAPS's primary responsibility is to support Marine (active and reserve) alcohol abuse prevention activities. Reviewing surrounding community reports detailing the current alcohol situation or other reports as appropriate is important. The AAPS, working with SACOs, supports the commander's prevention efforts by accomplishing the following:

(1) Performing an annual alcohol abuse prevention needs assessment that includes identification of: the degree and nature of alcohol problems, target population having the greatest risk of abuse, risk and protective factors, existing resources, and effective methods to disseminate information.

(2) Developing an annual installation Alcohol Abuse Prevention Plan from information gathered from the needs assessment. The plan must include:

(a) Specific prevention and marketing goals, objectives and target dates (i.e., a Plan of Action and Milestones (POA&M), to ensure a positive plan outcome.

(b) Prevention supportive actions for each major command, (e.g., Division, Marine Logistics Group (MLG), Wing, Base, Depot, Station).

(c) Measures of Effectiveness (MOEs) to evaluate program effectiveness, (e.g., increased level of substance abuse prevention awareness, effectively train Building Alcohol Skills Intervention Curriculum (BASIC) train-the-trainers, BASIC was appropriately implemented within the unit).

(3) Submitting the needs assessment, plan, and MOEs for review and approval by commanders of major commands, (e.g., Division, MLG, Wing, Base, Depot, Station), prior to publication.

(4) Submitting annual prevention plan outcomes to respective commanders in memorandum format for comments and utilization to adjust the following year's plan.

(5) Establish and provide a monthly BASIC train-the trainer course at the installation SACC per the prevention plan and as requested. HQMC (MRC-4) will provide BASIC course materials and training to establish the installation train-the trainer course.

(6) Assisting SACOs/Ss with unit prevention efforts.

(7) Training unit SACOs/Ss quarterly using a HQMC (MRC-4) approved course.

(8) Creating, preparing, reviewing, and maintaining materials for use in alcohol abuse prevention, such as lesson plans, resource guides and films.

(9) Disseminating alcohol abuse educational materials to military and civilian personnel on an as-needed basis.

(10) Establish an alcohol abuse prevention coalition comprised of personnel who have the ability to positively influence the annual alcohol abuse prevention plan, which may include the Provost Marshal's Office (PMO), Combat Operational Stress Control (COSC) Coordinators, DDRCs, Single Marine Program representatives, Recreation Specialists, Sexual Assault Prevention and Response (SAPR) personnel, PAOs, Semper Fit representatives, Substance Abuse Counselors, general counselors, and others.

k. Drug Demand Reduction Coordinator (DDRC). Installation DDRC responsibilities and DDR funding are limited to Marine Corps (active and reserve) illicit drug use prevention activities (e.g., DDR budget, illicit drug use education, and urinalysis). DDRCs are not to conduct treatment. Working with the installation AAPS and SACOs/SACSs, the DDRC supports the commander's drug use prevention efforts by accomplishing the following:

(1) Performing ongoing illicit drug use prevention needs assessment that includes identification of: the degree and nature of the drug problem, target population having the greatest risk of abuse, risk and protective factors, existing resources, effective methods of disseminating information, and perceived drug use norms. Reviewing surrounding community reports detailing the current drug situation or other reports as appropriate is important.

(2) Developing an annual plan from information received during the annual needs assessment. The plan includes:

(a) Specific prevention and marketing goals, objectives and target dates (i.e., a POA&M) to ensure a positive plan outcome.

(b) Prevention supportive actions for each major command (Division, MLG, Wing, Base, Depot, Station).

(c) MOEs to evaluate program effectiveness, (e.g., increased level of illicit drug use prevention awareness, number of SACOs trained, and urinalysis testing rates).

(3) Submitting the needs assessment, plan, and MOEs for review and approval by commanders of major commands.

(4) Submitting annual prevention plan outcomes to respective commanders in memorandum format for comments and utilization to adjust the following year's plan.

(5) Providing illicit drug use prevention education per the prevention plan and as requested.

(6) Assisting SACOs/SACSs with unit prevention efforts.

(7) Training unit SACOs/SACSs using a HQMC (MRC-4)-approved course.

(8) Creating, preparing, reviewing and maintaining materials for use in the illicit drug use prevention program, such as lesson plans, resource guides, and films.

(9) Participating in national anti-drug campaigns, such as the National Family Partnership's Red Ribbon Week, that encourage Marines, families, and citizens to lead healthy, drug-free lifestyles.

(10) Disseminating illicit drug use educational materials to military and civilian personnel and their families.

(11) Participating as a member of the alcohol abuse prevention coalition.

Chapter 2

Substance Abuse Prevention

1. Prevention Awareness Education and Training

a. Prevention awareness education is the foundation of any Substance Abuse Prevention Program. In the Marine Corps, the primary purpose of prevention education and training is to enhance mission readiness and provide requisite knowledge of the effects of alcohol and drug abuse, to ultimately assist in making responsible decisions. A secondary purpose is to train military and civilian supervisors in the important role of eliminating alcohol abuse and illegal drug use.

b. A thorough prevention awareness education program must address the entire scope of alcohol and drug abuse, both legal and illegal. Interactive participation will be used as much as possible to involve Marines in guided discussions and skill-oriented education beyond basic understanding. While education alone is not the answer to preventing abuse, if properly conducted, it can provide potential and present abusers with information to clarify personal values, improve problem-solving and decision-making skills, and understand alternative lifestyle choices. HQMC (MRC-4) will develop and publish a bi-annual prevention campaign plan. Tools such as these help commanders combat alcohol and drug use.

c. Unit commanders will ensure Marines at all levels receive prevention awareness education and training at least annually. Lesson plans and training assistance are available through Substance Abuse Counseling Centers (SACCs) or DDRCs.

(1) Officer Candidate and Recruit Training. The Commanding General (CG), Training and Education Command (TECOM) shall provide alcohol and drug abuse prevention training to officer candidates and recruits during initial training. The purpose of this orientation is to foster an understanding of the Marine Corps policy regarding alcohol and drug abuse. Training includes, at a minimum, the learning objectives listed below. Marine Corps schools develop and present alcohol and drug abuse prevention education as part of the course curriculum. The course of instruction is taught at the level of the audience. HQMC (MRC-4) will assist in lesson plan review and modification/development annually.

(2) Officer, Staff Noncommissioned Officer (SNCO), and Civilian Supervisory Training. Officers and SNCOs shall receive alcohol and drug abuse prevention training for supervisors annually. Course objectives are listed below. Civilian employees in supervisory positions of Marines are trained upon assumption of duties and every two years thereafter. In addition to supervisory training, commanders will identify two SNCOs or officers to receive BASIC train-the-trainer training at the installation SACC. Once trained, these individuals will train and support NCOs in the utilization and delivery of the BASIC course, as defined in the paragraph below. Commanders will maintain two trained individuals at all times.

(3) Noncommissioned Officer (NCO) Training. NCOs shall also receive annual supervisory training. In addition, special training through a HQMC approved course is required. BASIC is the only course available to meet this requirement. NCOs will use BASIC to train their subordinates on alcohol abuse prevention annually. Course objectives are listed below. BASIC is a one-time requirement for NCOs.

d. Training Objectives. Unit Substance Abuse Control SACOs/SACSs will seek support from subject matter experts (local law enforcement, DDR, SAPR, Semper Fit, COSC) to provide training on the objectives below.

(1) To state the Marine Corps policy on alcohol and drug abuse and dependence. Definitions of alcohol and drug abuse and dependence are found in Appendix A.

(2) To facilitate guided discussions on the risks associated with irresponsible drinking.

(3) To state the importance of recreational activities as alternatives to alcohol and drug abuse.

(4) To state the early warning signs and progressive nature of alcohol and drug abuse.

(5) To state the supervisor's role in setting a positive example, preventing alcohol abuse, identification and referral of abusers and alcohol abuse or dependency recovery.

(6) To describe the Marine Corps policy on illegal drug use and urinalysis.

(7) To recognize that alcohol and drug abuse contributes to domestic abuse, financial difficulties, and sexual assault,

and that alcohol and drug abuse is a mechanism used to cope with Combat Operational Stress (COS).

e. BASIC Course Objectives

(1) To state the impact of alcohol abuse on mission readiness.

(2) To state the role of the unit leader in preventing alcohol abuse.

(3) To state how alcohol is absorbed, processed, and eliminated from the body.

(4) To define Blood Alcohol Level (BAL), identify factors that influence BAL, and explain the effects of alcohol at various BALs.

f. Overseas Alcohol and Drug Abuse Orientation. All Marines will receive a prevention brief within five days of arrival at an overseas location. This brief emphasizes local laws, ordinances, and customs related to alcohol and illegal drug use. Each installation DDRC, unit SACO or substance abuse counselor is responsible for delivery of this briefing.

2. Alternative Activities. Another key element of a successful prevention program involves reinforcing the importance of alternative activities in preventing alcohol or drug abuse.

a. The long-standing perception that a "hard drinking" Marine constitutes part of the image of a "hard charging" Marine must be dispelled. Commanders must ensure all Marines understand consumption of alcohol is not essential or equal to Marine Corps pride. Activities should not be held which encourage drinking. Rather, drinking responsibly shall be the consistent goal. This policy, when combined with the attitude that alcohol abuse constitutes unacceptable behavior, is essential to the success of a prevention program.

b. A commander's responsibility to combat alcohol and drug abuse is not restricted to the installation. Cooperative efforts between military and civilian prevention programs should be aggressively pursued. All commanders should encourage their Marines to engage in non-drinking events and productive off-duty activities. Recreational opportunities must provide a change from the normal routine and a means of reducing stress and combating boredom. Marines have skills and interests which can be put to productive and constructive use during off-duty hours, to include tutoring, mentoring, coaching sports, involvement in youth programs, and volunteer fire and rescue service.

3. Deterrent Measures. Deterrent measures are necessary to support prevention programs and enhance personal and mission readiness. All commanders will utilize specific measures to deter substance abuse, including:

a. Publishing specific command policy deterring alcohol and drug abuse, to include consequences for misuse upon assumption of command.

b. Announced and unannounced health and comfort inspections of billeting areas and work spaces.

c. Random vehicle checkpoints by the installation PMO to deter driving while intoxicated. Checkpoints should not be limited to access points, but employed throughout the installation.

d. Aggressive random urinalysis testing.

e. Use of drug detection dogs during random vehicle checkpoints by PMO and health and comfort inspections.

f. Setting a positive example by all leaders in preventing alcohol abuse. Maintaining an atmosphere of "it's okay not to drink" is critical. Accordingly, leaders must ensure their attitudes and behaviors are consistent with Marine Corps policy and are above reproach.

g. Establishing proactive measures readily available to commanders with control over local command policies with regard to club operations, social gatherings, and command recreational activities. Commanders should institute policies which support responsible alcohol consumption in all aspects of club and community recreational activities, including, but not limited to ensuring:

(1) Command operations or functions do not promote alcoholic beverages. Advertisements and sponsorship of command activities or events will not glamorize alcohol without responsible use messages.

(2) Functions where alcohol is the only beverage are not authorized; non-alcoholic beverages will be readily available, in equal proportion, at all times.

(3) Food is available whenever alcoholic beverages are served.

(4) Drinking contests and alcohol-related games are not allowed.

(5) Alcoholic beverages are not given as gifts or prizes.

4. Drug Testing Program

a. Urinalysis is a valid and reliable deterrent measure and means of inspecting personnel to assess command readiness. Commanders shall utilize the DOD Drug Testing Program (DTP) software to establish an aggressive compulsory illicit drug use testing program, ensuring systematic screening of all Marines annually, regardless of rank, for the presence of drugs. Additionally, unit commanders will direct testing at least ten percent of their population monthly under the "IR," or random selection premise code. No Marines shall be excluded from current testing, regardless of proximity of previous testing. Total leadership effort with full participation of all officers, SNCOs, and NCOs is required to effectively counter drug abuse. Only commanders and MOs may direct that a urine sample be taken to test for drug presence.

b. Testing shall not be conducted:

(1) On a predictable schedule;

(2) On a specific day each month;

(3) Immediately following receipt of urinalysis testing materials;

(4) Coincident with specific or periodic musters, such as liberty briefs.

c. The above requirement does not preclude participation in special testing;

(1) Brig staff is tested quarterly.

(2) Prisoners are tested as directed by their commander.

(3) Marines assigned to SACCs and as SACOs/SACs are tested monthly, except for Recruiting Command SACOs, which are tested quarterly and as directed by the commander. Marines

involved in the collection and shipment of urine, such as Urinalysis Program Coordinators (UPCs) and observers, are also tested monthly. Their samples cannot be shipped in the same batches they were responsible for collecting; they must be collected and shipped separately by qualified individuals, such as SACOs and UPCs from other units.

(4) Reservists shall be tested no later than 72 hours after the beginning of scheduled annual training or initial active duty training.

(5) Commanders shall direct testing of Marines reporting in from Permanent Change of Station (PCS), Unauthorized Absence (UA), and extended leave periods (exceeding five days) within 72 hours of arrival/return to the unit.

5. Urinalysis Testing Premise Codes. Urinalysis testing is authorized under the following premise codes:

a. With the Marine's consent (VO). A Marine suspected of unlawfully using drugs may be requested to consent to testing. Prior to requesting consent, the command should advise the Marine he may decline the test. Where practicable, consent should be obtained in writing. Article 31(b) of reference (b) states warnings are not required in such cases provided no other questioning of the Marine takes place. Further guidance concerning consent searches is contained in Military Rules of Evidence (M.R.E.) 311, 312, and 314 through 316, reference (c).

b. Probable Cause (PO). A urinalysis may be ordered per M.R.E. 312(d) and 315, reference (c), when there is probable cause to believe a Marine committed a drug offense and it will produce evidence of such an offense. Commanders are strongly encouraged to consult with a Judge Advocate regarding each probable cause determination.

c. Periodic Urinalysis Tests

(1) Random selection (IR). Random testing of work sections, groups (selected by last digit of Social Security Number (SSN), or all command members. Testing should be conducted on a routine basis to act as a deterrent.

(2) Unit (IU). Testing, random or otherwise, of an entire unit, sub-unit or identified segment of a command.

(3) Accession (NO). Testing of all personnel seeking initial accession into the Marine Corps or recalled to active

duty. All officer candidates and recruits are tested within 72 hours of arrival at the training site, under premise code NO. Officer candidates are randomly tested during training. Officer candidates and recruits who refuse to consent to testing or if the initial urinalysis is confirmed for the presence of illicit drugs, are processed for separation per reference (d). Furthermore, the appointment or enlistment of a person determined drug dependent at the time of such appointment or enlistment shall be voided and he will be released from the control of the Marine Corps.

(4) Command-directed (CO). Ordered by the commander whenever a Marine's behavior or conduct evokes a reasonable suspicion of drug use or whenever drug use is suspected within a unit. A command-directed examination may be ordered to determine competency for duty and the need for counseling, rehabilitation, or other medical treatment. The distinction between command-directed, probable cause and voluntary is very important if future disciplinary action is contemplated. Consultation with the command's staff judge advocate is highly encouraged before using this basis.

(5) Physician-Directed (MO). A military physician may order a urinalysis in connection with a competence for duty examination under M.R.E. 312, reference (c), and in connection with any other valid medical examination based on a command referral for suspected drug abuse. Consultation with the command staff judge advocate is also highly encouraged before using this basis. As with a command-directed examination, if misconduct is suspected, this basis could limit a command's ability to later prosecute the Marine at court-martial or separate with an other than honorable characterization of service.

(6) Official Safety, Mishap, Accident (AO). A commander may order a urinalysis in connection with a formally convened mishap or safety investigation for the purpose of accident analysis and the development of counter measures. This basis will not be used if any other basis listed above could apply.

(7) Rehabilitation/Treatment (RO). Testing conducted in conjunction with participation in a substance abuse treatment program for alcohol/drugs (as opposed to a medical detoxification or treatment program). If a urinalysis taken upon entry to or during treatment is positive, the SACC or treatment facility returns the Marine to the parent command for appropriate action.

(8) Service-directed and Other Service-Directed (OO). Testing directed by the Secretary of the Navy or the CMC. It is used for SACC personnel, Marines involved in the collection and shipment of urine samples, security personnel, reenlistments, brig staff, prisoners, reservists, and Marines reporting in from PCS, leave or UA. Testing dates are randomly selected.

6. Urinalysis Collection Process

a. The commander designates in writing responsible Marines as UPCs and observers who are thoroughly trained by attending the SACO course, or by the unit SACO. Training must be accomplished before personnel can engage in any aspect of the collection process.

b. The SACO/UPC will use the DTP software and ensure all materials and personnel are ready for the collection, and is accountable for collection site security and urine specimens. Training on utilization of the DTP is obtained through the SACO course. Further assistance can be obtained through the installation DDRC and HQMC (MRC-4). To acquire the latest approved version of DTP, visit https://iftdtl.amedd.army.mil. In addition, a standard chain of custody form must be used to submit specimens for testing. For Marine Corps urinalysis collection, DD Form 2624, "Specimen Custody Document-Drug Testing" is used to document each batch submitted for testing. Specific instructions on completing the DD Form 2624 are found in paragraph 7 of this Order. DD Form 2624 should be marked "For Official Use Only" (FOUO) when filled in. If the form does not indicate FOUO when filled in, the users must stamp it on the form upon completion.

c. The unit UPC maintains a urinalysis ledger documenting all specimens collected with their identifying information as indicated below.

(1) Collection date (TIME/YEAR/MONTH/DAY). Each sample must have the same date per batch number.

(2) Batch number.

(3) Specimen number.

(4) Full SSN of the Marine providing the specimen.

(5) Testing premise code.

d. To begin the collection process, in a controlled area, the Marine presents a military identification card, and the UPC verifies the identity of the Marine. The identification card is retained by the UPC upon issuing the bottle and, if practical, should be placed in the empty urine bottle box slot used for shipping specimens until the bottle is returned after collection. The UPC will maintain strict control of the bottle when not in the hands of the donor. The UPC must ensure that bottles are separated in order to prevent confusion of specimens.

e. Specimens must be collected in full view of the observer. UPCs may also serve as observers. Observers shall:

(1) Be the same sex as the Marine providing the specimen.

(2) Witness the complete collection process (Marine urinating into the specimen bottle, placing the lid on the bottle, and delivering it to the UPC). The observer must maintain full observation of the specimen bottle while under his cognizance.

(3) Print his name and sign the urinalysis ledger certifying the specimen bottle contains urine provided by the Marine and there was no opportunity for substitution or adulteration.

(4) Ensure specimens provided by females are collected in a medical specimen container and transferred to the standard specimen bottle for processing. This transfer is done by the Marine providing the specimen in full view of the observer.

f. The UPC ensures the specimen bottle contains a minimum volume of 30 milliliters (mls), approximately one-third full.

g. Upon completion of the collection process, the UPC ensures the gummed label for each bottle contains the following:

(1) Collection date (YEAR/MONTH/DAY).

(2) Batch number (locally derived four-digit code assigned to each batch of 12 specimens or portion thereof).

(3) Specimen number (pre-determined two-digit sequential numbers assigned to each specimen in a batch).

(4) Full SSN of Marine providing specimen.

(5) Testing premise code.

(6) Initials of Marine providing specimen.

h. The label is attached to the bottle by the Marine (never put the Marine's rank, name, or signature on the label).

i. The Marine providing the specimen validates the specimen bottle by: verifying the identifying information on the label by printing his name and signing the ledger, and initialing the label with the initials of the name used in the ledger. If the Marine refuses to sign, verification of the specimen may be done (signed and initialed) by the observer and witnessed by the UPC and annotated in the comments section of the ledger. The UPC initials the label and prints his name and signs the ledger.

j. The Marine places tamper resistant tape across the cap of the specimen bottle. The tape must touch the bottle label on both sides of the bottle. The tape is transparent and will not obliterate any portion of the label. Then the Marine initials the tape on the bottle top. If the tape breaks, put another piece of tape over the broken tape, initialing the new tape. If the bottle leaks, the Marine transfers his urine into another unopened specimen bottle, under the direct observation of the observer, repeats the labeling and taping process and annotates the comments section of the ledger.

7. Instructions for Completing DD Form 2624. In addition to the following instructions, further training in completing this form can be obtained through the SACC.

a. Do not mark in areas labeled alphabetically; these are for laboratory use only.

b. Provide information from the urinalysis ledger in the numbered blocks only.

c. Abbreviated instructions for block information are provided on the back of the form. Instructions are as follows:

d. Block 1. SUBMITTING UNIT. Type the unit's Naval message Plain Language Address, and command phone number at the bottom of the block.

e. Block 2. ADDITIONAL SERVICE INFORMATION. Not required.

f. Block 3. BASE/AREA CODE. Not applicable to the Marine Corps; leave blank.

g. Block 4. UNIT IDENTIFICATION CODE (Reporting Unit Code). In the left block separate from the other five blocks, type or print "M." Enter the Reporting Unit Code of the unit submitting collected specimens in the remaining five blocks.

h. Block 5. DOCUMENT/BATCH NUMBER. A four-digit number generated by the DTP and assigned to each batch of 12 samples, or portion thereof. When DTP is not utilized due to unusual circumstances, a batch number is manually generated, starting with 0001-9999.

i. Block 6. DATE SPECIMEN COLLECTED. Enter the date in the following format: the year as a four digit number in the YYYY blocks, the month as a two digit number in the MM blocks, and the day as a two digit number in the DD blocks (place a zero in the left block if month or day is a single digit number).

j. Block 7. SPECIMEN NUMBER. Use the pre-printed numbers on the form to itemize specimen bottles. The form is designed to record a maximum of 12 specimen numbers.

k. Block 8. SSN. Enter the SSN of the Marine providing the specimen in the number sequence corresponding to the specimen number in block 7.

l. Block 9. TEST PREMISE. Enter the premise code indicating the reason for collection. DD Form 2624 requires two letter premise codes.

m. Blocks 10 and 11. TEST INFORMATION and PRESCREEN. For laboratory use only.

n. Errors. If information entered in blocks 7 through 9 has errors or will not be submitted as part of that batch, the entry must be voided. To void the entry, a black line will be drawn from the left border through the middle of the erroneous line in block 7 across blocks 8 and 9. The UPC dates and initials the right end of the drawn line. Only the remaining valid entries with their corresponding bottles are submitted as that batch.

o. Block 12. SIGNATURE AND CHAIN-OF-CUSTODY. UPCs shall use blocks 12 (a) and (b) to document the initial chain of custody. Block 12 (c) is completed when transfer to a storage locker occurs or other shipment status is known (e.g., shipped

U.S. Mail). Block 12 (d) documents the purpose of the transfer. If there are additional custody transfers, each must be documented in Block 12 (a, b, c and d) until the shipment is delivered to the laboratory.

p. Block 13. DAMAGE TO SHIPPING CONTAINER/DISCREPANCIES. For laboratory use only.

8. Collection Circumstances. If a Marine arrives after the testing period, the commander will be notified for decision on collection. Additionally, if a Marine cannot provide a specimen during the prescribed collection period or submits less than 30 mls, he is required to remain under observation in a controlled area, and to drink fluids normally consumed in the course of daily activity, not exceeding a total of twelve ounces, until he is able to provide a specimen, or the balance of an incomplete specimen. If the Marine cannot provide the balance of the specimen in the same bottle at the end of the collection period, the bottle is labeled, sealed with tamper resistant tape on the bottle top and initialed by the Marine and sent to the laboratory with the collection. The urinalysis ledger is annotated in the comments section that the specimen had "minimum volume." **No specimens are discarded from a collection due to insufficient volume.**

9. Preparation and Shipment of Urinalysis Specimens

a. The UPC/SACO ensures each box is enclosed in a leakproof secondary container, which contains sufficient absorbent material to absorb the entire contents in case of leakage.

b. The original DD Form 2624 is properly completed for each batch and attached to the outside of the box. A copy of the form is enclosed in the specimen box.

c. The UPC/SACO signs and dates the seal of the shipping container to ensure integrity of specimens. This requirement applies to all transportation methods, including hand-carried specimens.

d. Each shipping container is clearly marked on the outside "Clinical Specimens - Urine Samples."

e. Primary shipment modes are through regular United States Postal Service (USPS) mail or direct hand delivery to DoD-certified Navy Drug Screening Laboratories (NDSLs). The USPS is not required to sign for the shipment. Acceptance into the USPS should be noted by date stamp on the DD Form 2624 and a copy retained by the UPC/SACO. If the shipment requires a DD Form 1384, "Transportation Control and Movement Document," indicate a "priority one" on the form. On the U.S. Government Bill of Lading, the shipment is "priority one," indicated in the "description of contents" block. On DD Form 2624, the UPC/SACO enters one of the modes below in Block 12(d).

(1) "Released to United States Postal Service." Registered mail is not recommended.

(2) "Released to (Marine's rank/name) to hand-carry to drug screening laboratory." The Marine signs block 12(c) of the DD Form 2624 upon receiving the specimens.

(3) If boxes of specimens from several commands are collected at a central point for shipment, the actions described above are performed by the collection point coordinator after signing the DD Form 2624 in block 12(c) and providing a copy to the unit coordinator.

f. Urine specimens do not require refrigeration or freezing before shipment. However, each specimen should be forwarded for testing expeditiously, and provided with incontestable security and chain of custody measures while awaiting shipment. All specimens collected will be shipped for testing.

10. Urinalysis Collection Materials. The items below should be obtained through the supply system to ensure they comply with domestic and international mail carrier regulations.

a. Shipping Boxes

Stock Number	U/I	Size	Bottle Number
6640-00-165-5778	10	8"X3.5"X6"	12 bottles
(*) 8115-00-290-5494	25	8"X5"X4.5"	for 9 bottles
(*) 8115-00-290-3365	25	8"X4"X4"	for 6 bottles

(*) containers do not include bottles or separators

b. Mailing Pouches

Stock Number	Item	Size	Used for
6530-01-304-9762	mailing pouch	10.5"X15"	12 bottle box mailer

c. Absorbent pads for secondary container bags or mailing pouches:

Stock Number	Item	Size	Used for
6530-01-304-9754	pouch, liquid absorbent	5"X5"	single bottle or mailer

d. Stock Number Item

6530-00-837-7472, female specimen cup

e. Tamper resistant tape is recommended.
Vendor: TIME MEDICAL LABELING SYSTEM
144 Tower Drive
Burr Ridge, IL 60521
(800) 323-4840 or (800) 382-3371 (CA only)
Unit of issue: pad; 500 strips per pad
GSA contract number: GS-14F-01500
Product Number: TRL-2N

The National Stock Numbers (NSNs) for collection materials may change; update information accordingly.

11. Navy Drug Screening Laboratories (NDSLs). All units shall use DoD-certified NDSLs for testing.

a. Units east of the Mississippi River and overseas commands (except WestPac) will submit urine samples to NDSL Jacksonville, at the following address:

Commanding Officer
Navy Drug Screening Laboratory
Naval Air Station
Jacksonville, FL 32212-0113

b. Units west of the Mississippi River and WestPac commands will submit samples to NDSL San Diego, at the following address:

Commanding Officer
Navy Drug Screening Laboratory
34425 Farenholt Avenue Suite 40, Bldg 26-2b
San Diego, CA 92134-5298

12. Anabolic Steroid Testing. Possession or trafficking of anabolic steroids by Marine Corps personnel is prohibited and is considered a violation of reference (b), Article 112a, except as prescribed by a physician for therapeutic purposes and recorded in the medical record. All steroid samples must be submitted through NDSL San Diego, regardless of geographical location.

NDSL San Diego will then submit the samples to the contract laboratory for testing.

a. Samples submitted for testing must include a command letter, submitted on letterhead, including a command point of contact, e-mail address and phone number. Specimens for steroid testing may also be submitted for standard drug testing, however, this additional testing must be specifically requested by the submitting unit. Each specimen MUST be at least 60 mls.

b. Steroid sample collection follows the same procedures and documentation as required for normal drug testing.

c. There is no cost to the command for testing. Funding for testing is from a centralized annual budget maintained by NDSL, San Diego, and is limited to $25,000 Marine Corps-wide. This limits testing to command-directed and probable cause testing only. Units desiring to test more than ten samples should coordinate approval for testing through HQMC (MRC-4) via the DDRC or SACC. Only after proper coordination with the DDRC or local SACC will a command send the specimen(s) to the laboratory.

d. Each specimen is forwarded for testing expeditiously to the NDSL, San Diego address listed above.

13. Deceptive Devices/Methods. Per reference (e), the utilization of deceptive devices/methods is prohibited, and may result in punitive action under reference (b) or adverse administrative action or both. Per reference (e), deceptive devices/methods are intentionally used to avoid providing a urine sample when lawfully directed, to dilute a urine sample to reduce the quantitative value of that sample, to substitute any substance for one's own urine, or to chemically alter, adulterate or modify one's own urine to avoid detection of any controlled substance, or to assist another in attempting to do the same.

14. Command Confirmation

a. The legality or illegality of drug presence in a Marine's urine must be determined by the commander. Using all available information, including urinalysis results, the MO's review of medical and dental records, the Service Record Book (SRB), and chain-of-custody information, the commander shall make one of the following determinations.

(1) The Marine is an illegal drug abuser. All commanders shall process for separation per the guidelines contained in reference (d). A drug-related incident or wrongful use of a substance occurs when, in the commander's judgment, the preponderance of the evidence establishes the Marine used, abused, possessed, manufactured, or trafficked a controlled substance, prescribed medication, or an over-the-counter substance, pharmaceutical compound, and/or chemical. All confirmed incidents, civilian or military, of illegal drug use or possession are recorded in the Officer Qualification Record (OQR) or SRB per reference (f).

(2) The Marine is not an illegal drug abuser. In cases where the commander determines the urinalysis results involved an administrative error, such as faulty local chain-of-custody, or evidence of tampering, or the drug use was not wrongful (e.g., prescribed medication), the Marine shall not be identified as a drug abuser. The positive urinalysis is not a drug-related incident in such cases and no administrative or disciplinary action will be taken or any documentation of the case retained.

b. The commander provides results of every command confirmation, via memo, to the installation DDRC/SACC. The DDRC/SACC enters the results into the IFTDTL database, ensuring removal of results, if necessary, and maintaining accurate information on all Marines determined positive by the drug screening laboratory. All command confirmation memos must be maintained by the DDRC and will remain active as part of the unit SACO record for a period of two years following the last entry. Per reference (i), SSIC 5355, records of drug abuse are to be cut off and destroyed five years after the end of the calendar year the record is closed. After this period, they are destroyed by shredding or burning. Records of drug dependence, per reference (i), are retired to the nearest Federal Records Center when three years old.

15. Urinalysis Sample Retest

a. When a sufficient quantity of a specimen is available, the laboratory conducts a retest when:

(1) Requested by the submitting command,

(2) Requested by an administrative board under applicable board rules; or

(3) Upon order of a court-martial under applicable court-martial rules.

b. A Marine may request a retest at a civilian laboratory approved by DOD at his expense when a sufficient quantity of the specimen is available for retesting. A written request from the Marine via the chain-of-command is forwarded to the laboratory that conducted the initial test. The request must identify an approved civilian laboratory that will perform the analysis. Any NDSL can provide a list of approved laboratories.

c. The laboratory retains chain-of-custody documents and other paperwork for two years. The laboratory also retains positive specimens in a frozen state for one year and then discards them unless the submitting command requests to retain the specimen for an additional period of time.

16. Evidentiary Use of Urinalysis Results. Commands shall not order urinalysis tests for the primary purpose of obtaining evidence for trial by courts-martial or for other disciplinary purposes. However, urinalysis results may be used for any purpose, including disciplinary action and characterization of service in separation proceedings. If the test result is used in a court-martial or administrative separation proceeding, and the proceeding cannot be completed within a one-year period, the submitting command must request in writing an extension of the sample retention period from the Department of Defense (DOD)-certified laboratory that performed the test(s). Whenever urinalysis is conducted in the following situations, the results may be used as evidence in disciplinary proceedings under reference (b) and/or in administrative separation proceedings, including determination of character of service. Reference (d) addresses administrative discharge procedures.

a. An inspection under Military Rules of Evidence (M.R.E) 313 of reference (c) including health and comfort inspections, random selection, and unit sweeps;

b. Search and seizure under M.R.E. 315 (probable cause) of reference (c) or

c. An examination conducted for a valid medical purpose under M.R.E. 312(f) of reference (c). This includes emergency medical treatment, periodic physical examinations, and medical examinations for diagnostic or treatment purposes.

17. Expert Witnesses. Adjudication of confirmed drug abuse may require testimony of an expert witness. Expert witnesses

required for testimony on the forensic testing process conducted in urinalysis are requested from the nearest DOD-certified laboratory. In a case regarding the integrity of the specimen (e.g., tampering, adulteration), where the processing laboratory personnel are required, commands may request an expert witness from that laboratory. Commands must ensure all travel arrangements and related expenses are provided for expert witnesses.

Chapter 3

Substance Abuse Treatment

1. General. Per reference (e), the Marine Corps is required to identify, counsel, or treat Marines identified as alcohol or drug abusers or alcohol or drug dependent. Under no circumstances will a substance abuse treatment program established under the authority of this Order be degrading or employed which acts to segregate or degrade the individual Marine. All normal Marine Corps standards of conduct, customs, and courtesies will be observed. Degrading actions are contrary to the Marine Corps zero tolerance policy on hazing. Key program elements are timely identification, early intervention, effective treatment, rehabilitation, and appropriate disciplinary or administrative actions, followed by restoration to full duty or separation as appropriate.

a. In all substance abuse incidents, the Marine is assessed by the unit SACO, counseled by the unit commander, disciplined under reference (b), if warranted, and referred to the nearest SACC, or other service equivalent for screening in a timely manner.

b. Substance abuse intervention and treatment will be conducted at base, station, or depot SACCs by qualified personnel (e.g., ADC-II) certified Substance Abuse Counselors, physicians, and psychologists, with requisite skills and training). Treatment will be provided under the supervision of a MO (physician or clinical psychologist).

2. Substance Abuse Counseling Center Responsibilities

a. The SACC provides alcohol and drug abuse treatment to include screening, early intervention, comprehensive biopsychosocial assessments, and individualized treatment using a continuum of care model. A screening is a one-time occurrence; subsequent issues require re-evaluation or additions to the assessment. SACC outpatient services will be designed to address the individual's needs and to achieve permanent changes in drug/alcohol use behaviors. Inpatient services will be provided at military hospitals.

b. Initial Screening. SACC screenings are conducted using NAVMC 11700, and should take no longer than 60 minutes. This screening assists counselors, clinical staff, and medical personnel in making a determination on the degree of a problem and required services. If the need for an assessment is ruled out, the Marine is placed in an Early Intervention Program or returned to duty.

c. Assessment. A Marine requiring an assessment is assigned a case manager, also known as the primary counselor. The counselor, through a collaborative effort with the Marine, conducts a comprehensive biopsychosocial assessment, NAVMC 11692, of treatment needs. The counselor and the Marine use the results to develop an ITP. The Counselor's Assessment and Recommendation, NAVMC 11703, documents recommendations for services. The Counselor's Assessment Notes, NAVMC 11694, are a synopsis of the assessment. A form for the significant other, NAVMC 11701, is also filled out to assist with the assessment. A signed Consent Form, NAVMC 11691, must be obtained from the Marine prior to presenting this form to the significant other. On occasion, interviews and treatment sessions may be audio or videotaped, and/or observed. The purpose of these procedures is to provide quality professional services and for use in training Substance Abuse Counselors. An Audio/Video Acknowledgment form, NAVMC 11690, must be completed by the Marine. The Information Release Authorization form, NAVMC 11702, grants permission to release information contained in the Marine's treatment record to specific individuals or organizations. All aforementioned forms are located at https://navalforms.daps.dla.mil.

d. ITP. An ITP, NAVMC 11697, is developed through a collaborative effort between the Marine and the counselor. The treatment plan must be approved by the MO. ITPs contain clinical problems and agreed upon goals and objectives to be addressed in treatment. Target dates for achieving objectives are identified. Alcohol or drug abuse or dependency is a diagnosis and should not be confused with or listed as a problem on the ITP. The ITP is reviewed at least weekly and revised to reflect changes in treatment status. If goals are accomplished on the target dates, the plan continues as designed. If the Marine is encountering difficulties adhering to the ITP, the plan is reassessed and the treatment approach modified, if warranted, requiring approval by the MO. An ITP cover sheet (NAVMC 11696) is used to annotate diagnostic information and identified problems, providing clinical supervisory personnel a snapshot of problems and treatment direction.

e. Continuum of Care Portals of Entry. Patient placement will be based on the seven continuums of care dimensions and admission and discharge criteria below, not the drug and alcohol diagnosis. Assessment information, dimensions and placement criteria will be used by the Case Manager and the IDT to recommend the Marine's placement to the MO. Placement is the least intensive portal of entry that accomplishes treatment objectives while providing safety and security for the Marine. A Marine may enter the continuum of care at any portal.

(1) Early Intervention (EI). EI provides alcohol and drug abuse education to explore related risk factors, and assist in recognition of the consequences of inappropriate alcohol or drug use. Services are delivered in a classroom setting or in one-on-one sessions for a minimum of three hours. A Marine may be referred for an assessment, if new problems appear.

(2) Outpatient Services (OP). SACC OP services address the Marine's needs and achieve permanent changes in alcohol or drug use behaviors. OP services provide alcohol and drug education and counseling in regularly scheduled sessions of fewer than nine contact hours per week, until the treatment plan is complete. Appearance of new problems may require referral to other treatment or agencies. Length of services varies according to the severity of the illness and response to treatment.

(3) Intensive Outpatient Services (IOP). IOP services are designed for Marines requiring a more intensive treatment program while still meeting the patient placement criteria for OP care. Such services provide essential alcohol and drug education and treatment components while allowing the Marine to apply newly acquired skills within "real world" environments. Length of stay varies according to the severity of the illness and response to treatment, normally nine or more, but less than 20 contact hours per week, until the treatment plan is complete. Appearance of new problems may require referral to other treatment settings or agencies.

(4) Residential Services. Residential services are for Marines who meet the required patient placement criteria. Length of stay varies with the severity of the illness and response to treatment.

f. Interdisciplinary Team. The SACC Director assembles an IDT, at least weekly, to review the biopsychosocial assessment, ITP, and treatment. The IDT makes treatment recommendations to the MO. The MO makes the final decision on all clinical recommendations. The IDT consists of appropriately trained individuals able to assess, intervene, and treat alcohol and drug problems, (e.g., physicians, Substance Abuse Counselors, Social Workers, and nurses), the MO, and the primary counselor.

3. Patient Placement Dimensions. The seven placement dimensions are:

a. Acute Intoxication/Potential for Withdrawal. What risk is associated with the current level of acute intoxication? Is there a risk of withdrawal or seizures, based on previous history, as well as the amount, frequency, chronicity and recency of discontinuation or significant reduction of alcohol or drug use? Are there current signs of withdrawal? Does the Marine have support to assist in ambulatory detoxification, if medically safe?

b. Biomedical Complications. Are there current physical illnesses, other than withdrawal, that need to be addressed because they create risk or may complicate treatment? Are there chronic conditions that may affect treatment?

c. Emotional/Behavioral Complications. Are there current psychiatric illnesses or psychological, behavioral or emotional or cognitive problems that need to be addressed because they create risk or complicate treatment? Are there chronic conditions that affect treatment? Do emotional, behavioral or cognitive problems appear to be an expected part of the addictive disorder or do they appear to be autonomous? Even if connected to the addiction, are they severe enough to warrant specific mental health treatment? Is the Marine able to manage the activities of daily living? Can the Marine cope with emotional, behavioral or cognitive problems?

d. Readiness to Change. Does the Marine understand change needs to occur to improve the current situation? Is the Marine willing to attempt change or explore the relationship between alcohol and drug use and negative consequences? Are there any internal or external motivators?

e. Relapse, Continued Use or Continued Problem Potential. Is the Marine in immediate danger of continued severe mental health distress and/or alcohol or drug use? Does the Marine have any recognition of or skills in coping with, addiction problems to prevent relapse, or continued use? How severe are the problems and further distress that may continue or reappear if the Marine is not successfully engaged in treatment? How aware is the Marine of relapse triggers, ways to cope with cravings, and skills to control the impulse to use or the impulse to harm oneself or others?

f. Recovery/Living Environment. Are there family members, significant others, living situations or school or working situations that pose a threat to treatment engagement and success? Does the Marine have supportive friendships, financial resources, or educational or vocational resources that can increase the likelihood of successful treatment? Are there legal, vocational, Social Services or criminal justice mandates that may enhance motivation for engagement in treatment? Are there transportation, childcare, housing or employment issues that need to be clarified and addressed?

g. Operational Commitment. Does the command operational tempo allow for participation in the recommended treatment? If not, determine which level of care supports the Marine and mission. For alcohol or drug dependence, was action taken for admission into a residential program?

4. Admission Criteria

a. EI

(1) Dimensional Admission Criteria. The Marine who is appropriately cared for in EI meets one of the specifications in Dimensions 4, 5, or 6. Identifiable problems in Dimensions 1, 2, or 3 are stable or are addressed through appropriate OP medical or mental health services.

(2) Dimension 1, Acute Intoxication/Withdrawal Potential. No risk of withdrawal under the Withdrawal Assessment Scale (W.A.S.), NAVMC 11693, at <10. The W.A.S. allows counselors to evaluate and monitor withdrawal or intoxication problems to determine if services can be provided at a less intensive level of care or if the condition worsened to a point where more intensive services are required. A score greater than ten indicates more intensive monitoring or detoxification is required.

(3) Dimension 2, Biomedical Conditions and Complications. Biomedical conditions, if any, are stable or are actively addressed and will not interfere with therapeutic interventions.

(4) Dimension 3, Emotional, Behavioral or Cognitive Conditions and Complications. Emotional, behavioral or cognitive conditions and complications, if any, are addressed through appropriate services and will not interfere with therapeutic interventions.

(5) Dimension 4, Readiness to Change. The Marine expresses willingness to understand how current alcohol or drug

use may be harmful or impair the ability to meet responsibilities and achieve personal goals.

(6) Dimension 5, Relapse, Continued Use or Continued Problem Potential. Status is characterized by (a) or (b):

(a) The Marine does not understand the need to alter the current pattern of alcohol or drug use to prevent harm that may be related to such use; or

(b) Needs to acquire skills to change current pattern of use.

(7) Dimension 6, Recovery Environment. Status is characterized by (a) or (b) or (c) or (d):

(a) The Marine's social support system is not conducive to treatment success.

(b) Family member(s) currently is/are abusing alcohol or drugs (or has/have done so in the past), heightening the risk for a substance-related disorder; or

(c) The significant other(s) express(es) values concerning alcohol or drugs that create serious personal conflict; or

(d) Condone(s) or encourage(s) inappropriate use of alcohol or drugs.

b. OP. Dimensional Admission Criteria. The Marine who is appropriately admitted to OP treatment is assessed as meeting specifications in all of the following dimensions:

(1) Dimension 1, Acute Intoxication/Withdrawal Potential. No risk of withdrawal under the W.A.S. at <10.

(2) Dimension 2, Biomedical Conditions and Complications. Status is characterized by biomedical conditions and problems, if any, which are sufficiently stable to permit participation in OP Treatment.

(3) Dimension 3, Emotional, Behavioral or Cognitive Conditions and Complications. Status in OP Treatment is characterized by (a) or (b) or (c) below:

(a) No symptoms of a co-occurring mental disorder, or symptoms are mild, stable, fully related to substance use, and do not interfere with the ability to focus on treatment issues; or

(b) Mental status does not preclude the ability to:

1. Understand the information presented and

2. Participate in the treatment planning and process; or

(c) The Marine is assessed as not posing a risk of harm to self or others and is not vulnerable to victimization.

(4) Dimension 4, Treatment Acceptance/Readiness to Change. Status is characterized by one of the following:

(a) Awareness and acceptance of the addiction and commitment to recovery is sufficient to expect maintenance of a self-directed recovery plan, based on the following evidence:

1. Ability to recognize the severity of the alcohol or drug problem;

2. An understanding of the self-defeating relationship with alcohol or drugs;

3. Application of skills to maintain sobriety in a mutual or self-help fellowship and/or with post-treatment support care; and

4. The Marine does not meet any of the continued service criteria in this or another dimension that indicate the need for further OP treatment.

(b) The Marine consistently failed to achieve essential treatment objectives despite ITP revisions, to an extent that no further progress is likely.

(5) Dimension 5, Relapse, Continued Use or Continued Problem Potential. The Marine is assessed as able to achieve or maintain abstinence and related recovery goals, or to achieve awareness of a substance abuse problem and related motivational enhancement goals, only with support and scheduled therapeutic contact to assist in dealing with issues including, but not limited to, concern or ambivalence about preoccupation with alcohol or drug use, cravings, peer pressure and lifestyle and attitude changes.

(6) Dimension 6, Recovery Environment. Status is characterized by (a) or (b) or (c):

(a) The psychosocial environment is sufficiently supportive that OP treatment is feasible. For example, the significant other agrees with the recovery effort; there is a supportive work environment or legal coercion; adequate transportation to the program is available; and support meeting locations and non-alcohol or non-drug-centered work are near the home environment and accessible; or

(b) The Marine does not have an adequate primary or social support system, but demonstrates motivation and willingness to obtain such support; or

(c) The family, guardian, or significant other are supportive but require professional interventions to improve the chance of treatment success and recovery. Such interventions may involve assistance in a limited setting, communication skills, a reduction in rescuing behaviors, and the like.

c. IOP

(1) Dimensional Admission Criteria. Direct admission to IOP treatment is advisable for the Marine who meets specifications in Dimension 2 (if biomedical conditions or problems exist) and in Dimension 3 (if emotional, behavioral or cognitive conditions or problems exist) as well as in one of Dimensions 4, 5 or 6.

(2) Transfer to IOP treatment is advisable for the Marine who (a) meets the essential treatment objectives at a more intensive level of care and (b) requires the intensity of services provided at IOP treatment in at least one dimension.

(3) A Marine may be transferred to IOP treatment from OP treatment when OP treatment proves insufficient to address needs or when it consists of motivational interventions to prepare for participation in a more intensive level of treatment.

(4) Dimension 1, Acute Intoxication/Withdrawal Potential. No risk of withdrawal under the W.A.S. at <10 of this Order.

(5) Dimension 2, Biomedical Conditions and Complications. Conditions and complications, if any, are stable or are being addressed concurrently and will not interfere with treatment.

(6) Dimension 3, Emotional, Behavioral or Cognitive Conditions and Complications. Status is characterized by one of the following:

(a) Marine engages in addiction-related abuse or neglect of spouse, children or significant other, requiring IOP treatment to reduce the risk of further deterioration; or

(b) Has a diagnosed emotional/behavioral disorder which requires monitoring and/or management due to a history indicating its high potential for distracting from recovery or treatment such as a stable borderline personality or obsessive/compulsive personality disorder; or

(c) Is at mild risk of behaviors endangering self, others or property (e.g., suicidal or homicidal thoughts, but no active plan), but these are not serious enough to require 24-hour supervision.

(7) Dimension 4, Treatment Acceptance/Readiness to Change. Status is characterized by one of the following:

(a) Structured therapy and a programmatic milieu to promote treatment progress and recovery is required because of failure of motivating interventions at different levels; such interventions are not likely to succeed in an OP service; or

(b) The Marine's perspective inhibits the ability to make behavioral changes without clinically directed and repeated structured motivational interventions. For example, the Marine attributes alcohol or drug problems to other persons or external events rather than to a personal addiction. Such interventions are not feasible or are not likely to succeed in an OP service. Resistance, however, is not so high as to render the treatment ineffective.

(8) Dimension 5, Relapse, Continued Use Potential. Despite active participation at a less intensive level of care, the Marine is experiencing an intensification of addiction symptoms such as difficulty postponing immediate gratification and related drug-seeking behavior and is deteriorating in functioning, despite ITP revisions.

(9) Dimension 6, Recovery Environment. Status is characterized by (a) or (b):

(a) Continued exposure to the current work or living environment will render recovery unlikely. Resources or skills are lacking in order to maintain an adequate level of functioning without IOP Treatment; or

(b) The Marine lacks social contacts, or has inappropriate contacts that jeopardize recovery, or has few friends or peers who do not use alcohol or drugs. Resources or skills to maintain adequate functioning are lacking without IOP Treatment.

d. Residential Treatment. Refer to the facility admission requirements.

5. Continued Service and Discharge Criteria

a. Patient Placement Criteria. During the assessment, problems and priorities are identified as justifying admission to a particular level of care. Resolution of those problems and priorities determines when a Marine can be treated at a different level or discharged. The appearance of new problems may require services that can be provided effectively at the same level, or they may require a more or less intensive level. After the admission criteria for a given level are met, the criteria for continued service, discharge or transfer from that level are as follows:

(1) Continued Service Criteria: It is appropriate to retain the Marine at the present level if:

(a) The Marine is making progress, but has not yet achieved the goals articulated in the ITP. Treatment at the present level is as necessary to permit continued work toward treatment goals; or

(b) The Marine is not yet making progress, but has the capacity to resolve problems, and is actively working toward the goals articulated in the ITP. Treatment at the present level is assessed as necessary to permit continued work toward treatment goals; and/or

(c) New problems are identified that are appropriately treated at the present level of care. This level is the least intensive at which new problems can be effectively addressed. To document and communicate readiness for discharge or need for transfer to another level, each of the six dimension criteria should be reviewed. If the criteria apply to existing or new problem(s), the Marine should continue in treatment at the present level. If not, refer to the Discharge/Transfer Criteria below.

(2) Discharge/Transfer Criteria. It is appropriate to transfer or discharge the Marine from the present level if the following criteria are met:

(a) Goals articulated in the ITP are met, resolving problem(s) that justified admission to the present level; or

(b) The Marine is unable to resolve the problem(s) that justified admission to the present level, despite amendments to the ITP. Treatment at another level or type of service is indicated; or

(c) The Marine did not demonstrate the capacity to resolve problem(s). Treatment at another level or type of service is indicated; or

(d) The Marine experienced an intensification of problem(s), or developed a new problem(s), and can be treated effectively only at a more intensive level.

(e) To document and communicate the readiness for discharge or need for transfer to another level, each of the six dimension criteria should be reviewed. If the criteria apply to existing or new problem(s), the Marine should be discharged or transferred, as appropriate. If not, refer to the Continued Service criteria.

6. Case Management. Case management is an essential element of this model, beginning with assessment and ending with discharge planning. Every Marine assigned to treatment (OP, IOP, and Residential) is assigned a case manager. Case management involves identifying, coordinating, and documenting resources to assist in achieving goals outlined in the ITP. All case management decisions, as with treatment planning, must be discussed with and agreed upon by the Marine. Counselors document problems and outcome of referrals to other agencies on the Disposition of Referred Problems form, NAVMC 11698.

7. Assignment to Treatment Services

a. Marines requiring medical detoxification will not enter any treatment program until detoxification is completed. The need for medical detoxification will be determined only by a MO.

b. Marines with drug/alcohol problems will be treated locally whenever possible to allow for family and command participation in the treatment program. When treatment is provided outside the local area, Marines are not allowed to drive their Privately Owned Vehicles (POVs). Drug dependent Marines will be treated in residential programs at Naval Hospitals when deemed to be the most appropriate care by the MO.

c. Commanders will issue a Letter of Assignment to Marines scheduled for treatment services. This letter will clearly state the type of program to which the Marine is assigned, reason for assignment, program goals, expected behavior during treatment, and consequences of refusing treatment or failing to successfully complete the program. A copy of this letter will be included in the individual's unit and SACC record.

8. Medical Evacuation (MEDEVAC) System. The MEDEVAC system will be used when determined by the MO to be the most beneficial transportation protocol.

a. The SACC, working closely with the patient's command, will contact the nearest patient affairs office to obtain a bed assignment and arrange for MEDEVAC to the treatment facility.

b. Marines attending treatment outside the local area will require no cost Temporary Additional Duty (TAD) orders.

9. Treatment Failure. A Marine who fails to make progress in treatment or aftercare, or who regresses, should not automatically be considered a treatment failure. If the outcome indicates a need to modify the ITP, the plan is reassessed by the SACC, and modifications are made so the Marine can effectively achieve the assigned goals. However, a Marine who refuses, fails to participate, or does not successfully complete treatment or aftercare and is determined a treatment failure by a MO, will be returned to his command and processed for separation per reference (d).

10. Separation and Retention

a. Regardless of the type of discharge, all commanders will ensure that no Marine requiring treatment is separated until the treatment process is completed. This does not include aftercare. Upon completion of treatment, the treatment facility will advise the Marine of his Veterans' Affairs (VA) substance abuse treatment eligibility.

b. Before deciding to separate a Marine, the commander should consider all possible factors, to include the needs of the Marine and the Marine Corps. Often, a developing alcohol problem manifests itself in a series of acts of misconduct and/or steadily deteriorating performance. Every effort must be made to identify and treat Marines before their record has deteriorated to the point where administrative separation is likely.

c. Any Marine deemed to be a treatment failure by a physician or psychologist credentialed and privileged through the Naval Hospital shall be processed for separation per reference (d). Likewise, any Marine who returns to the abuse of alcohol and/or whose standards of conduct and performance declines following the successful completion of a treatment/aftercare program shall be processed for separation per this Order and reference (d), if determined not amenable or qualified for additional treatment.

d. Marines who have been retained, will be ordered into a treatment program recommended by the SACC, and comply with aftercare program requirements. Marines who were assigned to and complete outpatient or residential treatment may request reenlistment upon completion of a twelve-month observation period for performance and conduct. If the Expiration of Active Service (EAS) does not support the observation period, an extension may be granted for up to twelve months. The observation period shall begin on the date of treatment completion.

e. All alcohol-related incidents will be the subject of formal command counseling with the Marine involved. Commanders will direct an OQR/SRB entry be made after counseling for an alcohol-related incident. OQR/SRB entries and CMC-directed (DC) fitness reports are required for second and subsequent incidents of alcohol abuse. Whenever an entry is made in the OQR/SRB, the Marine must be given the opportunity to make a statement, if desired. See references (f) and (g).

11. Special Populations. Treatment will be provided to family members at least 18 years of age and retirees on a space available basis. Treatment is not authorized for family members under the age of 18. Additionally, treatment for aviators and other aircrew personnel requires procedures detailed in reference (h). More detailed procedures can be found in the current edition of the Naval Aerospace Medical Institute's Aeromedical Reference and Waiver Guide.

12. Voluntary Self-Referral for Drug Abuse Treatment. Per reference (e), all active duty and reserve Marines who self-refer for drug abuse to qualified representatives (anyone in the chain of command) shall be screened for drug dependency at a medical facility. Those who are diagnosed as drug dependent are exempt from disciplinary action, processed for administrative separation, and offered treatment. Personnel who are subsequently screened as "not drug dependent" are not exempt from disciplinary action and processed for separation.

13. Unit and SACC Individual Records

a. Unit SACO Records. The unit maintains a record on each Marine referred to the SACC for services. When not in use, records must be kept in a locked container. SACO files, including screening records, will be active for two years following the last entry. Per reference (i), records, with the exception of drug dependence records, are to be cut off and destroyed five years after the end of the calendar year the record is closed. After this period, they are destroyed by shredding or burning. Records of treatment for drug dependence will be retired to the nearest Federal Records Center when three years old. Unit SACO records will include a chronological log of incidents, evaluations, referrals, treatment, and aftercare progress. Information is kept in ordinary file folders clearly marked "Confidential Personal Information, for use by Commanding Officer, the SACO/S, and Treatment Personnel Only." These records have two parts: a document section (right side) and a client history (left side). When a Marine transfers, active records are forwarded to the gaining command, marked "For Commanding Officer's Eyes Only." Records shall consist of the following forms, found at the following website: https://navalforms.daps.dla.mil.

(1) Privacy Act Statement. Signed by the Marine, a one-time explanation of Privacy Act requirements as they relate to alcohol and drug treatment and associated records. This form is collocated with each form where a Privacy Act Statement is necessary.

(2) SACO Referral Information (NAVMC 11685). Completed by the Marine to assist the SACO in evaluating and recommending the Marine for referral to the SACC, via the commander, for screening and assessment.

(3) Supervisor Input (NAVMC 11686). Completed by the Marine's supervisor, this information is used by SACOs and

Substance Abuse Counselors to make an appropriate recommendation to commanders.

(4) Medical Record Review (NAVMC 11687). Medical information that aids in the SACC screening. The medical record review is completed by the SACC at the initial screening. Although the SACO may have knowledge of a Marine receiving medical care possibly related to substance use, screening individual medical records by the SACO is not recommended.

(5) Letter of Treatment Assignment. The commander issues this letter to the Marine, which clearly states the type of program to which the Marine is assigned, reason for assignment, program goals, expected behavior during treatment, and consequences of refusing treatment or failing to successfully complete the program. A copy of this letter is included in the unit and SACC records.

(6) Other Documents. All documents regarding any alcohol or drug abuse history shall be filed, in chronological order. Examples of appropriate documents are copies of PMO reports, duty log pages, emergency room reports, breath or blood analysis reports, and letters of treatment assignment and completion.

(7) Chronological Log (NAVMC 11695). The document section substantiates the information in this section. Entries must be thorough, detailed, and frequent enough to enable the commander and treatment personnel to familiarize themselves with the case. An entry is made for every event indicating an incident of abuse which could affect treatment progress. The SACO/S will meet with each Marine in aftercare at least bi-weekly and document progress in the record after every meeting. Only the SACO/S, commander, and Substance Abuse Counselor will make entries in a record.

b. SACC Screening and Treatment Records. SACCs are required to maintain records containing clinical forms to provide alcohol and drug treatment. All records, when not in use, will be in a locked container at all times. The information contained therein is highly personal and sensitive in nature and will not be transmitted outside the SACC, except as authorized by law or regulations. When a Marine transfers, active SACC records will be forwarded to the gaining Base/Station SACC. Records contain a client file identification form, progress notes, and the clinical package, and are clearly identified as alcohol and drug treatment records. Each active record will reflect a minimum of semi-weekly contact between the

Marine and counselor, unless special circumstances warrant more frequent entries. These entries, known as progress notes will contain the following:

(1) Date.

(2) A clear statement of the level and duration of client's treatment.

(3) A clear statement of any concerns, problems, or progress, which should be tied to the assessment dimensions and problem areas in the treatment plan.

(4) Any report of client statements or actions should be written in behaviorally descriptive terms.

(5) Any plan for client action should be tied to an assessment dimension and to a problem area in the treatment plan. This should be reflected in the treatment plan.

c. Records of alcohol abuse, alcohol dependence, drug abuse and drug dependence, including screening records, are active for two years following the last entry. Per reference (i) SSIC 5353, records of alcohol abuse and dependence are to be cut off and destroyed five years after the end of the calendar year the record is closed. After this period, they are destroyed by shredding or burning. Per reference (i), SSIC 5355, records of drug abuse will be cut off and destroyed five years after the end of the calendar year the case is closed. Per reference (i), SSIC 5355, records of drug dependence are transferred to the nearest Federal Records Center when three years old.

14. Aftercare

a. Upon treatment completion, the commander places the Marine in a unit aftercare program; services are not provided at the SACC. Aftercare requires monitoring and documentation of progress for a minimum of one year. The cognizant SACC or the residential treatment facility provides an Aftercare Plan, which varies for each person in order to meet individualized needs. Aftercare requires close observation and mandatory completion of the Aftercare Plan and participation in self-help groups such as Alcoholics Anonymous (AA) and Narcotics Anonymous (NA), when recommended by the SACC, for a Marine diagnosed alcohol or drug dependent. For more information on self-help groups, visit the AA website at http://www.aa.org. Participation in self-help groups is not mandatory for non-dependent abusers. The unit

SACO/S provides an accurate assessment of progress to the commander for the duration of the aftercare period.

b. A Marine diagnosed as alcohol dependent who returns to the use of alcohol, while in aftercare, is immediately counseled by the commander and referred to the nearest SACC for re-evaluation and recommendation. Likewise, a Marine not diagnosed as alcohol dependent, who returns to the abuse of alcohol requires immediate referral.

c. A Marine who returns to the abuse of alcohol and/or whose standards of conduct and performance declines following the successful completion of a treatment or aftercare program, is processed for separation per this Order and reference (d), if determined not amenable or qualified for additional treatment.

15. Declining Treatment. If a Marine processed for separation declines treatment, the command shall:

a. Provide in writing, the location of the Veterans Administration Medical Facility (VA MEDFAC) nearest their place of residence or home of record and document the date and the fact the Marine was provided this information in the record.

b. Document declination of treatment in the OQR/SRB, page 11, with the Marine's signature acknowledging the refusal. Commanders may note and sign the entry if the Marine refuses signature.

16. Veterans' Administration Medical Facility (VA MEDFAC)

a. The use of VA MEDFAC for treatment of drug/alcohol dependence is considered an alternative to treating the Marine at a MTF or SACC and should only be utilized for extraordinary circumstances. If a commander determines that treatment at a VA MEDFAC is in the best interest of the Marine Corps and the Marine being separated, approval must be obtained from CMC (MRC-4).

b. Marines treated at a VA MEDFAC will be separated from active duty through a designated Marine Corps activity per reference (j). Treatment will be at the VA MEDFAC with capabilities nearest the Marine's home of record or place of residence.

Chapter 4

Confidentiality

1. Disclosure of Confidential Information. Records of the identity, diagnosis, or treatment of any Marine, maintained in connection with the performance of any Marine Corps program or activity relating to substance abuse education, prevention, training, treatment, rehabilitation, or research, shall be confidential and may be disclosed only under the circumstances listed below.

2. Disclosure Outside the Uniformed Services. Disclosure of confidential client information outside the Uniformed Services is governed by references (k) and (l), and is permitted under the following circumstances:

a. With the prior written consent of the Marine, but only to such extent, under such circumstances, and for such purposes as may be allowed per reference (l). A "Consent to Obtain Information" form, NAVMC 11691, authorizes release of client information. When such a disclosure is made, the original copy of the release form is placed in the clinical file. This form allows the staff to obtain information from other programs that will assist with treatment efforts.

b. Whether or not the Marine, with respect to whom any given record referred to above is maintained, gives written consent, the content of such record may be disclosed outside the Uniformed Services:

(1) To medical personnel to meet a bona fide medical emergency.

(2) To qualified personnel conducting scientific research, management or financial audits, or program evaluation. Such personnel may not identify, directly or indirectly, any Marine in any report of such research, audit, or evaluation, or otherwise disclose client identities in any manner.

(3) If authorized by an appropriate order of a court of competent jurisdiction granted after application showing good cause therefore, including the need to avert a substantial risk of death or serious bodily harm. In assessing good cause, the court shall weigh the public interest and the need for disclosure against the injury to the Marine, to the physician-client relationship, and to treatment. Upon the granting of such order, the court, in determining the extent to which

disclosure of all or part of a record is necessary, shall impose appropriate safeguards against unauthorized disclosure.

(4) Prohibitions of this section do not apply to any exchange of records between the Uniformed Services and those components of the Department of Veterans Affairs furnishing healthcare to veterans.

3. Disclosure Within the Uniformed Services. Specific prohibitions contained in references (k) and (l) do not apply to the exchange of confidential client information within the Uniformed Services. Such disclosures, however, are subject to the limitations prescribed in this Order. For this section, the term "commander" is defined as those who possess Special Courts-Martial convening authority (normally Battalion or Squadron Commanders and above).

a. Consistent with reference (l), whether or not the Marine, with respect to whom any given record referred to above is maintained, gives written consent, the commander has access to all program records, including disclosures made to substance abuse treatment personnel, at AA or NA meetings, or while attending preventive education or intervention classes. However, the commander's use of such information is subject to the limitations prescribed in this Order.

(1) The commander is the only member of the command with access to confidential information. The Marine may also provide written consent to release the information to a specific member of the command. Notwithstanding the above, information which discloses a crime or illegal act is about to take place is immediately transmitted to the installation PMO for appropriate command notification and to facilitate the protection of potential victims.

(2) A "Confidentiality of Client Records," NAVMC 11689, must be signed to confirm an understanding of what a provider is required to immediately report to the commander, i.e., disclosure of a past crime or illegal act, an incident that places the command or its Marines in jeopardy, and all other matters significant to the command.

(3) Records of the identity, diagnosis, prognosis, or treatment of any Marine who sought or received counseling or treatment in any DON substance abuse treatment program, which are maintained in connection with such program, may not be introduced against the Marine in a court-martial except as authorized by a court order issued under the standards set forth

in reference (k). This restriction does not apply to the use of such records for rebuttal or impeachment purposes where evidence of illegal drug use or alcohol abuse (or lack thereof) was first introduced by the Marine.

(4) Disclosures made to treatment personnel relating to past substance use/abuse, or possession incident to such use/abuse, including disclosures made at AA or NA meetings, or when attending preventive education or intervention classes, may not be used against the Marine in any disciplinary action under reference (b) or as the basis for characterizing a discharge, provided the information is disclosed by the Marine for the purpose of seeking or obtaining treatment.

(a) This provision does not preclude the use of disclosed information to establish the basis for separation in a separation proceeding or to take other administrative action. Nor does it preclude the introduction of evidence for impeachment or rebuttal purposes in any proceeding in which illegal substance abuse (or lack thereof) was first introduced by the Marine.

(b) The use of information disclosed by a Marine to persons other than military substance abuse program personnel is not limited under this provision.

(c) Information disclosed in response to official questioning in connection with an investigation or disciplinary proceeding will not be limited under this provision.

(d) Confidential information may also be disclosed within the Uniformed Services, with or without consent, under the following circumstances:

1. To meet a bona fide medical emergency.

2. In communications between staff members within a program or between program staff of the same or different Armed Forces facilities and other qualified staff that provides program services.

3. When it contains no identifying data.

4. If authorized by an appropriate order of a court (or court-martial) of competent jurisdiction granted after application showing good cause therefore. In assessing good cause, the court shall weigh the public interest and the need for disclosure against the injury to the Marine, to the

physician-client relationship, and to treatment. Upon granting such an order, the court, in determining the extent to which disclosure of all or part of a record is necessary, shall impose appropriate safeguards against unauthorized disclosure.

b. Except as authorized by court (or court-martial) order under the above paragraph, no record of a Marine who sought or received treatment in a substance abuse treatment program, maintained in connection with such program, may be used to initiate or substantiate a criminal charge or to conduct an investigation of the Marine. However, such evidence may be used for rebuttal or impeachment purposes where evidence of substance abuse (or lack thereof) was introduced by the Marine and is otherwise admissible.

Chapter 5

Quality Assurance (QA)

1. General. The QA Program is an ongoing process to monitor and evaluate substance abuse prevention and treatment programs. SACC directors, AAPSs, and DDRCs will implement a QA Program to ensure effectiveness of all services.

2. QA Program Standards. The QA program requires the development of an annual QA plan, which addresses the following Headquarters Marine Corps Substance Abuse Program standards:

a. Prevention: 1) having timely prevention programs, including 2) conducting a needs assessment, 3) developing an annual prevention plan, and 4) meeting the needs of commanders,

b. Treatment: 1) having timely treatment programs, including 2) conducting screenings within five days of referral, 3) coordinating assessments and ITPs with the Marine and counselor, and 4) conducting treatment following the requirements in chapter 3 of this Order.

c. Annual QA outcomes, in written report format, will be published for review by all commanders.

3. QA Objectives

a. Assess and monitor the quality and appropriateness of services and identify opportunities to improve using a client-driven outcomes management system that solicits direct consumer feedback, encourages individualized service delivery, and enables ongoing monitoring of service effectiveness for providers.

b. Justify resources to maintain, and preferably exceed, the HQMC Substance Abuse Program standards.

c. Integrate, track, and trend QA information quarterly to identify patterns or processes, which may need in-depth review.

d. Identify prevention and treatment program weaknesses and improvement opportunities through data analysis and customer satisfaction surveys.

4. QA Requirements. The Program is guided by a plan which includes, at a minimum:

a. Program Objectives and Measures of Effectiveness (MOEs). In order to remain successful in meeting the needs of and providing services which benefit the community, it is important to assess program outcomes quarterly. To know the effectiveness of the program requires examination of several outcomes. Outcomes are indicators or measures demonstrating the extent to which program goals and objectives are achieved; thus, outcomes must be developed in conjunction with goals and objectives.

b. Organizational and program responsibilities.

c. Program scope including the methodology for obtaining customer feedback on quality of services. A blank follow-up evaluation form (NAVMC 11699) can be completed by the Marine's supervisor.

d. Required QA functions including what is to be done, by whom, and the frequency.

e. Information flow and review of needs. Specific need(s) and risk factors for groups of various pay grades which the program or service is intended to address. Services must be evaluated and assessed at least quarterly to accommodate changing populations and needs.

f. Annual review of program effectiveness with revision as necessary.

g. Program and service success is directly linked to its outcomes. Outcomes should be identified, routinely reviewed and integrated into day-to-day program management. Some important program indicators include:

(1) Ability to mitigate identified risk factors for varying targeted populations;

(2) Demand for preventions and treatment services;

(3) Level of satisfaction by commanders and Marines receiving services;

(4) Expected prevention and treatment outcomes of commanders and individuals;

(5) Program awareness by leaders and Marines;

5. Program Assessment. While not conclusive, this chart identifies elements to assess the effectiveness of Substance Abuse programs and services.

What You Want to Know	**Information Sources**	**What to Look For**
- Are Marines, family members and commands aware of your substance abuse prevention and treatment services? - Who is using the services? - Who is the program not reaching? - Are needs of the community and target groups being met? - What is the quality of services? - What are the results of services?	- Community Needs Assessment - Client feedback - Follow-up surveys - Intake forms - Interviews (SACOs) - Command leaders (commander, XO, SgtMaj, 1stSgt) - Command feedback - Focus groups - Customer satisfaction surveys - Installation or command statistics and incident reports	- Increase in self referrals for treatment services - Increased demand for prevention training - Change in perception of service quality - Individual impact (returned to full duty and completed enlistment) - Relapse rates - Command referrals - Incident rates; trends

Figure 5-1.--Program Assessment Chart

Appendix A

Definitions

1. Abuse. Misuse or wrongful use of a substance; whether or not used therapeutically, legally, or prescribed by a physician.

2. Addiction. A psychological and sometimes physical dependence characterized by a compulsive desire/need to use a drug or other substance on a continuous basis to experience its effects and/or avoid the discomfort of its absence.

3. Alcohol Abuse. Use of alcohol to an extent that it has an adverse effect on performance, conduct, discipline, or mission effectiveness, and/or the user's health, behavior, family, community, or the Marine Corps, or leads to unacceptable behavior as evidenced by one or more acts of alcohol-related misconduct. Alcohol abuse is also a clinical diagnosis based on specific diagnostic criteria delineated in the American Psychiatric Association's (APA) "Diagnostic and Statistical Manual (DSM) of Mental Disorders," current edition, and must be determined by a qualified MO or DOD-authorized licensed practitioner. A diagnosis of alcohol abuse generally requires some form of treatment.

4. Alcohol Dependence and/or Alcoholism. Psychological and/or physiological reliance on alcohol as indicated by evidence of tolerance or withdrawal characterized by the development of withdrawal symptoms 12 hours or so after the reduction of intake following prolonged, heavy, alcohol ingestion. People are alcohol dependent when abstinence from use impairs their performance or behavior. Alcohol dependence is a clinical diagnosis based on specific diagnostic criteria delineated in the current edition of the DSM, and must be determined by a MO or DOD-authorized practitioner. Untreated, alcohol dependence may lead to death.

5. Alcohol-Related Incident (ARI). An offense punishable under the UCMJ or civilian authority where, in the CO's judgment, consumption of alcohol was a contributing factor in misconduct, substandard performance, or the inability to perform an assigned mission.

6. Anabolic Steroids. Any drug or hormonal substance, chemically and pharmacologically related to testosterone (other than estrogens, progestins, and corticosteroids) that promotes muscle growth, and includes any salt, ester, or isomer of such a drug or substance described or listed in reference (m) if that

salt, ester, or isomer promotes muscle growth.

7. Controlled Substances. Chemical compounds, anabolic steroids or other substances included in reference (e).

8. Controlled Substance Analogue

a. Per section 802 of reference (m), except as provided in subparagraph 8.b. below, this term means a substance:

(1) The chemical structure of which is substantially similar to the chemical structure of a controlled substance in schedule I or II of reference (m):

(2) Which has a stimulant, depressant, or hallucinogenic effect on the central nervous system that is substantially similar to or greater than the stimulant, depressant, or hallucinogenic effect on the central nervous system of a controlled substance in schedule I or II of reference (m); or

(3) With respect to a particular person, which such person represents or intends to have a stimulant, depressant, or hallucinogenic effect on the central nervous system that is substantially similar to or greater than the stimulant, depressant, or hallucinogenic effect on the central nervous system of a controlled substance in schedule I or II of reference (m).

b. Such a term does not include:

(1) A controlled substance;

(2) Any substance for which there is an approved new drug application;

(3) With respect to a particular person any substance, if an exemption is in effect for investigational use, for that person, under Section 505 of the Federal Food, Drug, and Cosmetic Act (21 U.S.C. 355) to the extent conduct with respect to such substance is pursuant to such exemption; or

(4) Any substance to the extent not intended for human consumption before such an exemption takes effect with respect to that substance.

9. Designer Drug. Any substance which has a stimulant, depressant, or hallucinogenic effect on the central nervous system similar to or greater than the stimulant, depressant, or hallucinogenic effect on the central nervous system of a

controlled substance in schedule I or II of reference (m), regardless of the chemical structure of the substance or the duration of the effect.

10. Detoxification. A process to reduce or remove the toxic properties of drugs from the body. It is normally the first step in the alcohol or drug abuse treatment process and is designed to free the alcohol or drug addict of the habit.

11. DUI/DWI (Driving Under the Influence/Driving While Intoxicated). DUI/DWI refers to the operation of, or being in the physical control of a motor vehicle or craft while impaired by any substance, legal or illegal. Definitions vary slightly from state to state. In most states, a recorded BAL for alcohol of 0.08 is prima facie proof of DUI/DWI without other evidence. In many states, drivers can be considered impaired at levels lower than 0.08 and convicted on other evidence without a recorded BAL. Operation of, or being in physical control of a motor vehicle or craft with any recorded BAL by a person under the age of 21 may be prima facie evidence of DUI in many states.

12. Drug. Any chemical compound, which may be used on or administered to humans or animals, that modifies their physiological or psychological behavior or function.

13. Drug Abuse. Wrongful use of a controlled substance, prescription medication, over-the-counter medication, or intoxicating substance (other than alcohol) to an extent that it has an adverse effect on performance, conduct, discipline, or mission effectiveness, and/or the user's health, behavior, family, community, or the Marine Corps, or leads to unacceptable behavior as evidenced by one or more acts of drug-related misconduct. Drug abuse also includes the intentional inhalation of fumes or gasses of intoxicating substances with the intent of achieving an intoxicating effect on the user's mental or physical state, and steroid usage other than that specifically prescribed by a competent authority. Drug abuse is a clinical diagnosis based on specific diagnostic criteria delineated by the APA in the current edition of the DSM and must be determined by a qualified MO or DOD-authorized licensed practitioner. A diagnosis of drug abuse generally requires some form of treatment. See "wrongful."

14. Drug Abuse Paraphernalia. Equipment, products, and materials of any kind that are used, intended or designed for use in planting, propagating, cultivating, growing, harvesting, manufacturing, compounding, converting, producing, processing, preparing, testing, analyzing, packaging, repackaging, storing,

containing, concealing, injecting, ingesting, inhaling or otherwise introducing into the body a controlled substance, per reference (e). Drug abuse paraphernalia includes, but is not limited to:

a. Hypodermic syringes, needles and other objects used, intended or designed for use in injecting controlled substances into the body, and metallic or other containers used for mixing or other preparation of heroin, morphine, or other narcotic substances prior to such injection;

b. Objects used, intended or designed for use in ingesting, inhaling, or otherwise introducing controlled substances, such as marijuana or cocaine into the body, such as:

(1) Pipes, with or without screens, for smoking marijuana or cocaine with names such as chamber pipes, carburetor pipes, electric pipes, air driven pipes, chillums, bongs, ice pipes or chillers, hashish heads, punctured metal bowls, etc.;

(2) "Roach clips" or objects used to hold burning marijuana too small or short to be held in the hand;

(3) Cocaine spoons.

c. The words "equipment, products, and materials" should be interpreted according to their ordinary or dictionary meaning. To ensure that innocently possessed objects are not classified as drug abuse paraphernalia makes the criminal intent of the person in possession or control of an object a key element of the definition. Some evidentiary factors to consider in determining criminal intent, and hence whether an object is illegal drug abuse paraphernalia, are as follows:

(1) Statements by the person in possession or by anyone in control of the object concerning its use;

(2) Proximity of the object, in time and space, to the unlawful use, possession, or distribution of drugs;

(3) Proximity of the object to controlled substances;

(4) Residue of controlled substances on the object;

(5) Instructions, oral or written, provided with the object concerning its use;

(6) Descriptive materials accompanying the object that explain or depict its use;

(7) Existence and scope of legitimate uses for the object in the community; and

(8) Expert testimony concerning its use.

15. Drug Dependence. Psychological and/or physiological reliance on a chemical or pharmacological agent as such reliance is defined by the DSM. The physiological alteration to the body or state of adaptation to a drug which after repeated use results in the development of tolerance, and/or withdrawal symptoms when discontinued, and/or the psychological craving for the mental or emotional effects of a drug that manifests itself in repeated use and leads to a state of impaired capability to perform basic functions.

16. Drug-Related Incident. Any incident where the use of a controlled substance or illegal drug, or the misuse of a legal drug or intoxicating substance (other than alcohol) is a contributing factor. Mere possession or trafficking in a controlled substance, illegal drug, legal drug intended for improper use, or drug paraphernalia may be classified as a drug related incident. Additionally, testing positive for a controlled substance, illegal drug or a legal drug not prescribed, may be considered an unconfirmed drug-related incident.

17. Drug Trafficking. Wrongful distribution including sale or transfer of a controlled substance, and/or the wrongful possession or introduction into a military unit, base, station, ship, or aircraft of a controlled substance with the intent to distribute.

18. Illegal/Illicit Drugs. Drugs prohibited by law or lawful drugs when obtained or used without proper authority, to include abuse of otherwise legal drugs.

19. Inhalant Abuse (Huffing). Intentional inhalation or breathing of gas, fumes or vapors of a chemical substance or compound with the intent of inducing intoxication, excitement, or stupefaction in the user. Nearly all abused inhalants produce effects similar to anesthetics, which slow down the body's function. Varying upon the level of dosage, the user can experience slight stimulation, a feeling of less inhibition, loss of consciousness, or suffer from Sudden Sniffing Death

Syndrome. (This means the user can die from the first, tenth, or one hundredth time he or she abuses an inhalant.)

20. Marijuana or Cannabis. Cannabis is the plant commonly referred to as marijuana.

21. Narcotics. A class of drugs including, but not limited to: Opium, Morphine, Codeine, Heroin, Hydromorphone, Meperidine, Methadone, LAAM, Percodan, Darvon, and Talwin.

22. Prevention Program. An ongoing process of activities to counter the threat of alcohol and drug abuse in a geographical area or command. Prevention programs normally include: needs assessment, policy development and implementation, public information activities, education and training, deglamorization, and evaluation. Effective prevention programs are tailored to the specific area or command, i.e., command/community-based.

23. Recovering Alcohol Dependent. A person whose alcohol dependence is in remission and maintained through abstinence and participation in a recovery program.

24. Rehabilitation. Restoration of an individual to self-sufficiency through treatment, education, leadership, clinical counseling and aftercare.

25. Substance Abuse. A maladaptive pattern of substance use manifested by recurrent and significant adverse consequences related to the repeated use of the substance.

26. Substance Dependence. Cluster of cognitive, behavioral, and physiological symptoms indicating that the individual continues the use of the substance despite significant substance-related problems.

27. Tolerance. The need for greatly increased amounts of a substance to achieve intoxication (or the desired effect) or a markedly diminished effect with continued use of the same amount of a substance.

28. Withdrawal. A combination of symptoms that normally occurs when detoxifying from alcohol and certain drugs. It may include any and all of the following symptoms: intense anxiety, degrees of mental and physical impairment, tremors, convulsions, hallucinations, delirium, respiratory failure, and death.

29. Wrongful. Conduct prohibited by this Order is wrongful if it is done without legal justification, authorization, or

excuse. Wrongfulness includes use contrary to the directions of the manufacturer or prescribing healthcare provider.

Appendix B

Substance Abuse Program Flowchart

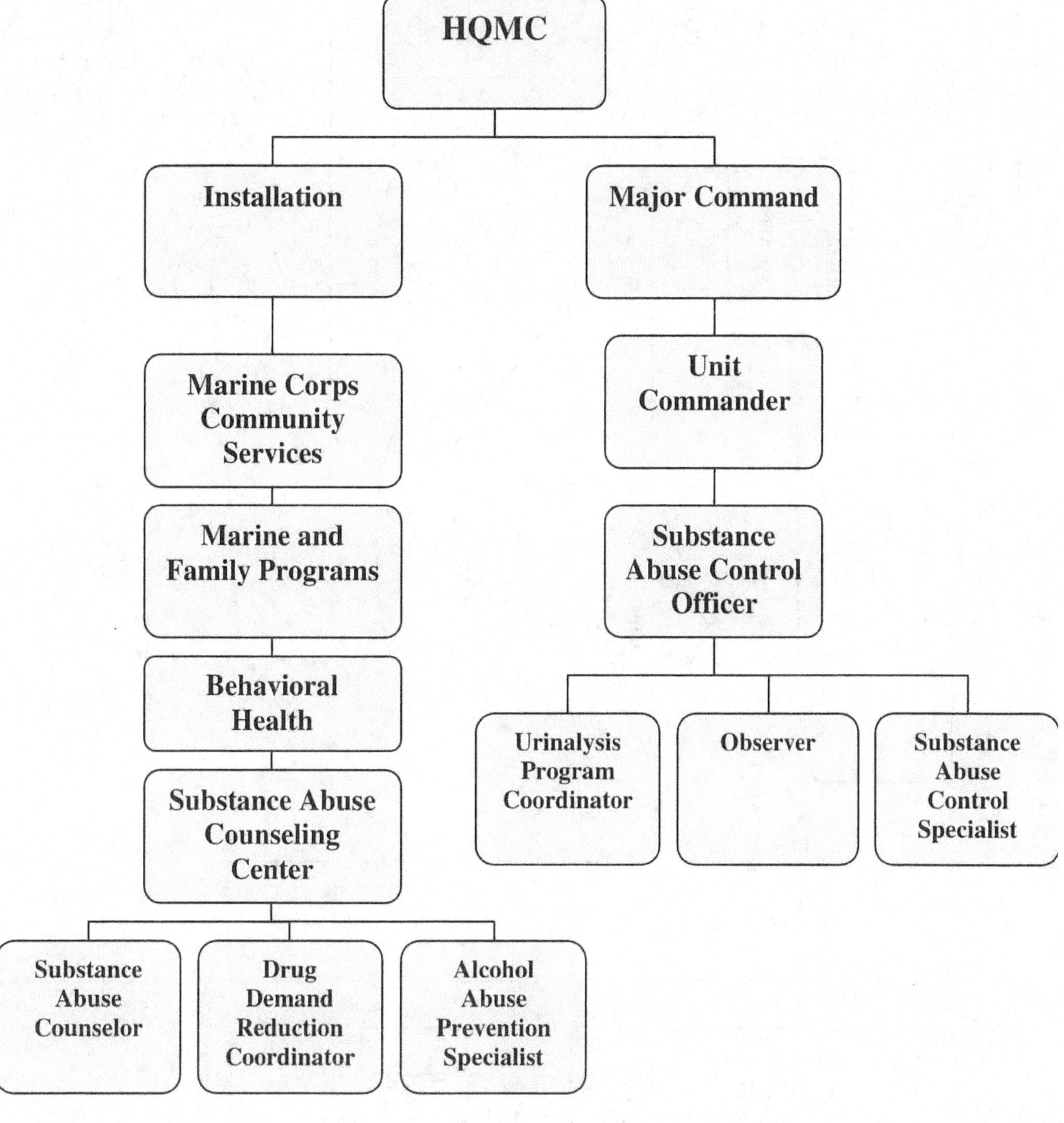

Patient Placement and Treatment Process

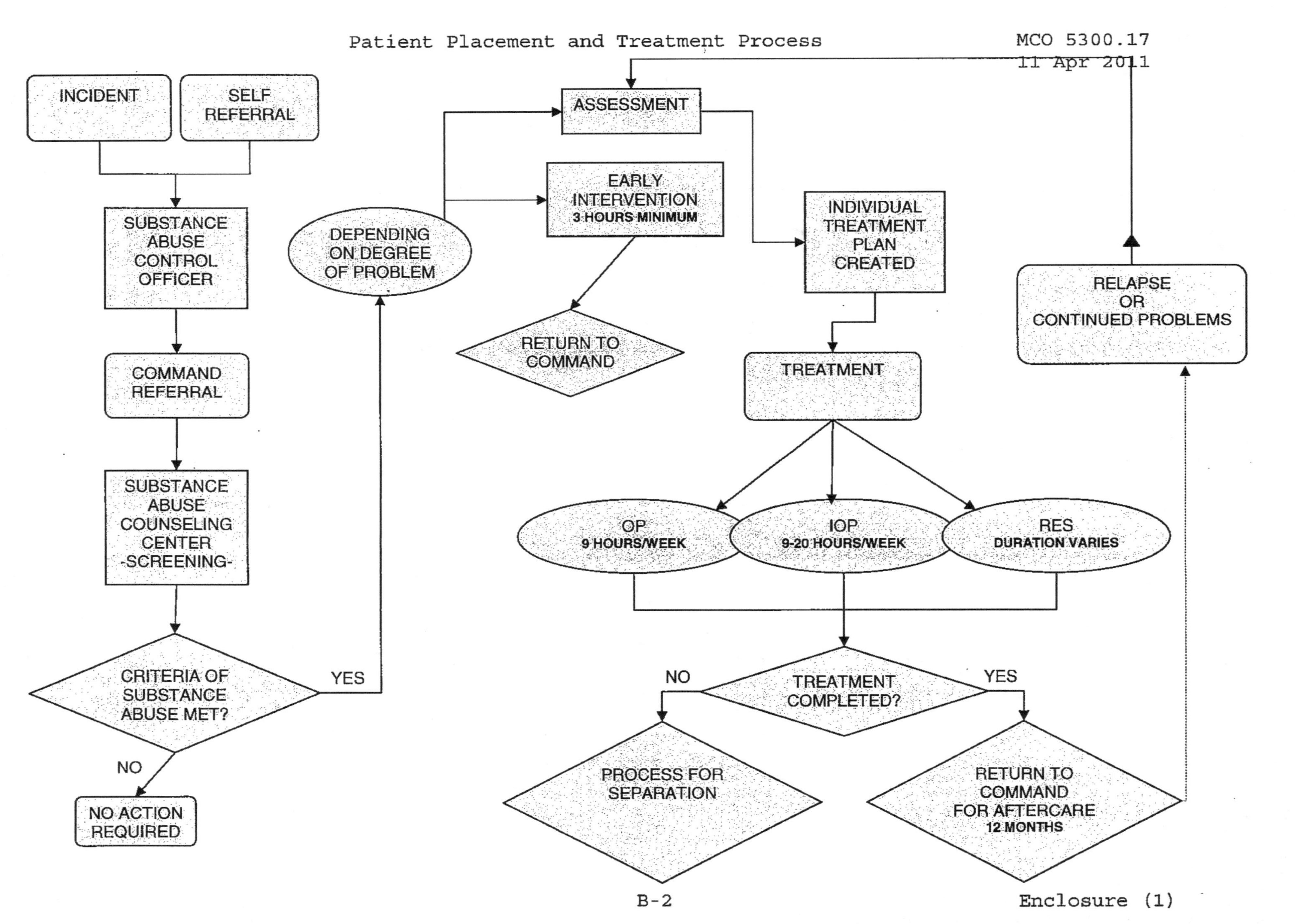

www.ingramcontent.com/pod-product-compliance
Lightning Source LLC
Chambersburg PA
CBHW081430310526
45790CB00020B/2293

* 9 7 8 1 4 9 0 4 0 4 5 6 1 *